TOO[
HOMESTEADS
PAST AND PRESENT

Rica Erickson
and
Robyn Taylor

HESPERIAN
PRESS

2006
HESPERIAN PRESS
P.O. BOX 317
VICTORIA PARK 6979
65 OATS STREET
CARLISLE 6101
WESTERN AUSTRALIA.
www.hesperianpress.com
books@hesperianpress.com

ISBN 0 85905 262 8

Cover: Glenfield, 1969. Painting by Pat Macknay.
Courtesy Pat Macknay.

Hesperian books are available direct from the publisher. For a full catalogue of Hesperian books on Australiana, natural history, pearling, military history, exploration, Aboriginal ethnography, bush verse and gold prospecting, please download from our website.If you do not have internet access please forward a self-addressed, stamped business size envelope (220 x 110) to the above address.

All Hesperian books are printed on quality paper and will not discolour with age. They are section sewn in signatures, the pages will not drop out and the binding will not crack. This book is made to last.

CONTENTS

Illustrations

Chapter

ILLUSTRATIONS

MAPS

PLANS

PHOTOGRAPHS
(Note: where no acknowledgement is made, the source of the
illustration is from Rica Erickson's collection)

ACKNOWLEDGEMENTS

Many people during the past sixty years have shared their family stories with Rica, knowing that they may be printed some time in the future. These contributors are too numerous to name here but they are listed in the endnotes. Special thanks are given to John Maslin for the maps and plans, Beth Field who contributed a number of her photographs, and Jenny Sinclair and Kim Watson for typing up the original manuscripts and Richard Taylor who undertook the index.

This book has been a labour of love for all.

The authors would like to thank the Toodyay Shire Council for permission to reproduce photographs from *A History of Toodyay* published by the Toodyay Road Board in 1949. We also thank the owners of the old homesteads recorded in this book who have been generous with information and for giving permission to photograph their homes.

INTRODUCTION

For well over a century after the Toodyay Valley was explored and opened for settlement in 1836, descendants of the pioneers in the district were still telling of the experiences of those early settlers. When the old farms passed from family hands their new owners welcomed authentic information about their early history.

The purpose of this book is to bring together the fascinating stories that surround these old farms, the lives of those who built and lived in them, and something of the class structures that prevailed at the time when bond and free worked to create their own destinies.

During the early years of settlement, the English observance of the upper, middle and lower classes of society was maintained, and the gentry were most prominent in shaping public affairs. Anyone who was imprisoned or entered a poor house, or even sought 'poor relief' lost respectability and was regarded as lower class.

With the transportation of convicts from 1850 to 1868 a fourth convict class was established and this became the largest in the colony. The colonists prior to this numbered less than 5000. During the period of transportation nearly 10,000 convicts and almost as many poor women migrants came to Western Australia. Few colonial women married expirees since the penalty would be exclusion from polite society. As a result the expirees usually married the women immigrants, thus creating an even larger proportion of the lower classes of the colony because most of their children almost inevitably married within the bond class.

This social structure prevailed until the end of the century when the gold rushes of the 1890s brought many thousands of people who regarded all men as equal, and for whom the class divisions had no significance.

These three periods of Western Australian history are easily defined. The early colonial years 1829 to 1849 were followed by the years 1850 to 1888 when the bond class had a significant effect on the economy. These were followed by the golden years, when sudden wealth thrust an isolated conservative colony into the bustle of the modern machine age.

The pastoral industry was dominant until the end of the 1800s. The transition to mining and farming during the early 1900s was dramatic and is easily traced in the Toodyay district.

The following stories of the farms and families are based upon the 1849 Census of the Toodyay district, as well as anecdotal contributions from many descendants of those early settlers.

CONVERSIONS

The Imperial measures of colonial days have been retained.

        1 acre = 0.41 hectares
        1 mile = 1760 yards = 1.61 kilometres
        1 yard = 3 feet = 0.91 metres
        1 foot = 12 inches = 30.5 centimetres
        1 inch = 2.54 centimetres
        1 gallon = 4.55 litres

Currency

        £1 = one pound = 1 sovereign = \$2
        20/- = 20 shillings = £1 = \$2
        12^d = 12 pence = 1 shilling

This currency has been inflated forty to fifty times which indicates that £1 in colonial years would be worth about \$100.

1. EXPLORATION AND EARLY SETTLEMENT

The Swan River Colony was established in 1829 as the first free settlement in Australia. The two other colonies that existed at this time were New South Wales, set up as a penal settlement in 1788, and Van Diemen's Land (Tasmania) which also served as part of the British convict system. The western part of the Australian continent was outside the boundary of these lands. Fearing foreign interests in the region Governor Darling of New South Wales sent a detachment of soldiers with a number of convicts to set up a garrison at King George Sound. They arrived on Christmas Day 1826. The garrison was subsequently withdrawn in 1831.

Formal possession of the western half of the continent to be known as the Swan River Colony had taken place in 1827 after Captain James Stirling encouraged Governor Darling to allow him to explore the Swan River region. Stirling's reports on the fertility of the soils and the availability of water were highly enthusiastic and it was eventually decided by the British government to establish a crown colony of free settlers on the Swan River. The settlers had to be prepared to pay their own way and provide all the necessary goods and chattels for their existence. In return, those who arrived before the end of 1829 would be allotted one acre of land for every 1s 6d they invested. Also 200 acres was granted for the passage of each labourer brought out by the settler. The allotted land had to be worked within 21 years or it would be forfeited. Free allotments also had to be selected by a given time. The prospect of land ownership and a new life led to what was dubbed 'Swan River mania'. For many it was a chance in a lifetime to aspire to the class of landed gentry.

By the end of 1830 over 1,100 settlers had arrived and there were 443 claims for free grants, totalling one and a quarter million acres. Soldiers, sailors, lawyers and doctors competed with merchants, agriculturalists, yeomen and artisans for land.

Captain Stirling had been appointed Governor of the new colony and in his Proclamation of Settlement he gave notice that the indigenous people were to be protected under British law. However, this protection did not extend to the protection of any sense of belonging they had to the land. They were a nomadic people and their 'ownership' was not recognized or understood in any British court of law. They soon became a displaced people with many choosing to live on the fringes of the new

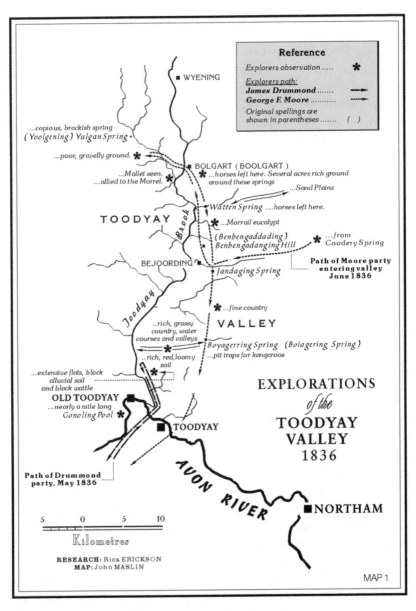

Toodyay Valley explorations, 1836.

2

settlements. Tragically, many were to die from introduced illnesses such as measles and whooping cough.

All the land along the Swan Valley was soon allocated. Some grants were also taken up in the Helena Valley to the south. The Surveyor-General's office was hard pressed to keep up with the demands of the new arrivals and this meant many allotments could not be properly surveyed or the nature of the land wholly understood before selection. It was soon discovered that the glowing reports by Stirling had been exaggerated. The soils of the coastal plain were sandy and largely infertile and water was not as plentiful as hoped. Farmers needed large tracts of good pastoral land and reliable sources of water. To this end attempts were made to explore the upper reaches of the Swan River but the valley narrowed into a rocky gorge as it entered the Darling Range to the east.

In 1830 Stirling sent out an exploratory expedition under the leadership of Ensign Robert Dale of the 63rd Regiment to find a way over the barrier of the Darling Range. Dale travelled up through the Helena River Valley and eventually came across a river which he named the Avon flowing through good pastoral lands. Subsequent expeditions during that year confirmed Dale's favourable reports on the Avon district and land was set aside for the distribution of land grants and the future towns of York, Beverley and Northam. During another expedition in 1831 Dale, accompanied by George Fletcher Moore the Advocate General, sighted the junction of the Toodyay Brook with the Avon River. The first land grants in this region were taken up in 1832 and a site for the town of Toodyay was set aside on the Avon, located several kilometers downstream of the present town of Toodyay.

Among the first claimants for land in this new Avon River region were J. Hardey and the Clarkson brothers, leading members of the Wesleyan community that had arrived in 1830 aboard the *Tranby*. Another was retired army officer Captain Francis Whitfield the Resident Magistrate at Guildford who already had land in the Helena Valley.

By 1836 the number of settlements along the Avon Valley from Beverley to Northam had increased to nineteen homesteads. These included John Morrell's 'Morby' near the Northam townsite and William Heal's 'Newleyine' further downstream. Several other grants had been selected beyond these properties but none were occupied. The nearest unselected land was in the vicinity of the Toodyay Brook. The time was approaching when colonists who had not claimed their free grants would have to forfeit them.

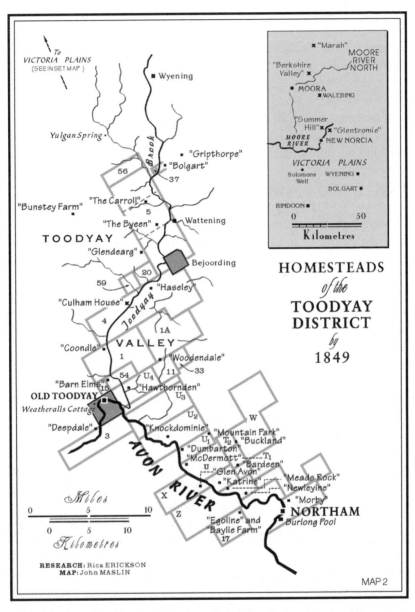

Homesteads in the Toodyay District and Moore River region by 1894.

In May 1836 James Drummond the botanist, Captain Francis Whitfield, the official leader of the party, and the partners Thomas and Alex Anderson set out from the Swan Valley for the Toodyay Brook. Drummond had successfully applied to have his land allocation in the Helena Valley exchanged for land in the Avon Valley, and chose an area around the Toodyay Brook. The party decided to take a shorter route than by way of York. Engaging a Canning River Aborigine named Babbing as a guide they saved about 30 miles of hard travel. Babbing took them by way of the Woorooloo and Jimperding brooks. Knowing others would eventually follow this route they blazed a trail by marking trees. They also noted the indigenous names for the waterholes.

When the party arrived at their destination they were pleased with the beauty of the valleys and the presence of water. Drummond recorded that he learnt from Babbing that the place was called Duidgee and that it was a favourite place of the Aboriginal people. He presumed this was because of its natural abundance. In subsequent accounts, such as the one published in the 17th September 1836 edition of the *Perth Gazette*, Drummond was credited with drawing attention to the 'Valley of the Toodyay' with its potential for a thriving settlement. As Babbing was out of his own territory the party could only spend one day inspecting the land they decided to claim.

On arrival back at Perth they learnt that Thomas Waters, a vigneron at Guildford, had already applied for land next to Drummond's grant along the Toodyay Valley. Also George Leake, a wealthy Perth merchant, had enlisted the help of G. F. Moore to explore further up the Valley. Leake had 14,000 acres yet to select, jointly for himself and his London associate named Richard Norman.

Moore's guide was a Swan River Aborigine named Tomghin. After the party lost sight of the track blazed by Drummond, Tomghin took them down a brook which Moore named Mistake Creek because it led instead to William Heal's 'Newleyine' grant. After visiting Morrell at Morby cottage, Moore and Leake engaged a Northam Aborigine named Hannapwirt to guide and protect them as they explored land to the east before turning to the Toodyay Valley. Hannapwirt guided them to the Toodyay Valley by entering it at Bejoording Springs. Moore learnt the names of many of the places they saw from Hannapwirt.

The party found cattle tracks at Bejoording which led up the Valley. From the top of a small conical hill named Benbengaddading they spied out the land and saw grassy slopes in every direction. They then rode between two hills, the steeper one was named Bedowan, and they soon came to the Bolgart Springs (Boolgart). Leaving their horses to graze there the men then walked north to Yulgan (Yoolgenning) through poor country and were disappointed to find the water was brackish. The next day they proceeded eastwards to Wattening Spring. Going further east across a stretch of dry sandplain they found the cattle. They were too shy to be approached so the men turned south to Jandaging Spring, a short distance east of Bejoording. They did not return to the Toodyay Valley but rode a further seven miles south to the Boiagering (Boyagerring) Spring. The horses were left there to graze while the men walked westwards through seven miles of attractive country, crossing what they assumed to be the Toodyay Valley. Returning to Boiagering Spring they then rode in a direct line to the Avon Valley and camped for the night beside a long deep pool.

Having bypassed the land in the Toodyay Valley that Drummond and Waters had already claimed, Leake's party returned to the Valley next morning to make a hasty inspection of land west of Boiagering. A heavy fog shrouded the country above the river flats, but they were satisfied with what they could see. On his return to Perth Leake applied for 14,000 acres next to Waters' boundary.

As soon as Alfred Waylen and Thomas Newte Yule heard about Leake's application, they applied for equally large areas beyond his claim, thus locking up the land beyond to Bolgart. On 30th June 1836 the editor of the *Perth Gazette* reported that 'almost the whole of the Toodyay Valley is held by four or five landholders'. In September Governor Stirling selected another large area to be known as 'Deepdale' down the Avon Valley from the ford at Toodyay.

In 1837 G.D. Smythe surveyed townsites at Toodyay and Bejoording and also a Water Reserve at Bolgart and placed survey posts on the summits of Benbengaddading and Bedswan (previously spelt Bedowan).

In 1838 Captain Francis Whitfield was appointed Resident Magistrate of the Toodyay district. He took up residence at his grant the following year after the boundaries of the Toodyay and York districts were defined.

By 1849 a Census of the Toodyay district listed 58 dwellings from 'Morby' to 'Berkshire Valley' representing fourteen homesteads on large grants and a number of shepherds huts and labourers' quarters. (Appendix 1) Each family required at least five acres of wheat while 25 acres sustained the largest establishments.

The cost of carting grain from Guildford was prohibitive so the wheat crops were very precious. These were endangered when Aborigines began their annual burning of the bush. This 'fire-stick' practice was to promote fresh growth to attract game such as kangaroo and wallaby. Also in summer the burning of bulrushes near swamps made it easier for their women to dig up the tubers that were a valuable source of food. To prevent the loss of settlers' crops, the Resident Magistrate offered the Aborigines wheat if they refrained from burning until after harvesting. This wheat was levied from the settlers and supplemented by the Governor with gifts of rice and also blankets for the older Aborigines. After the burns there was a shortage of feed for the settlers' flocks lasting for months.

By 1841, almost the whole of the Toodyay Valley was either owned or leased by three men - James Drummond, Squire Samuel Pole Phillips and Captain John Scully. They had no wish to trespass on each other's land, so in February 1841 they set out to explore the country about 40 miles to the north of Bolgart where they found good grazing and water along the Moore River. They named the area the Victoria Plains.

Before long they had sheep grazing there almost the whole year, apart from those times when the sheep were sent south for shearing or redrafting those for sale and to separate the lambs from the ewes. These isolated areas were Crown Land. Governor Hutt, newly in office, objected to Crown Land being used in this way and in 1845 a system of pastoral leases was introduced.

The flocks were cared for by shepherds who were set up in outcamps that were maintained by the flock owners. The shepherds had intimate knowledge of the best country. They owned some sheep of their own given in lieu of wages during the years when prices for wool were low. The pastoral lease system gave them the opportunity to secure large areas of land with pre-emptive right of purchase of small blocks of land around the water holes. In this way they soon had control over vast areas much larger than the largest grants.

In those days the northern boundary of the Toodyay district was not defined. The Resident Magistrate's census of 1849 included all households from 'Morby' near Northam to 'Berkshire Valley' beyond the Moore River. He listed temporary huts as well as established homesteads and named the head of each household giving the ages and sexes of the residents. Stock numbers were noted and also the areas of different crops under cultivation. This record offers a unique opportunity to study the social structure of the district. Those who cultivated large areas of wheat or owned large numbers of stock would be pastoralists of high standing. Those men with small areas of cultivation and a few head of stock could

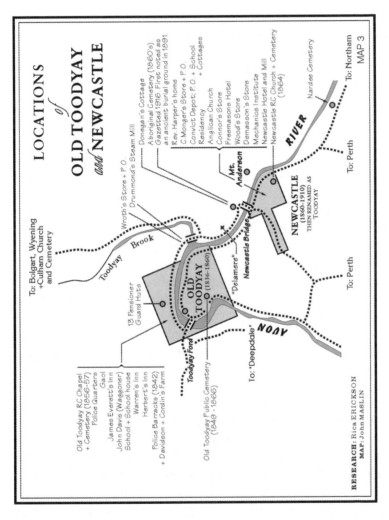

LOCATIONS
of
OLD TOODYAY and NEWCASTLE

To: Bolgart, Wyening +Culham Church and Cemetery

Old Toodyay RC Chapel + Cemetery (1856-57)
Police Quarters
Gaol
James Everett's Inn
John Davis (Waggoner)
School + School house
Warren's Inn
Herbert's Inn
Police Barracks (1842)
+ Davidson + Cordin's Farm

Old Toodyay Public Cemetery (1849 - 1866)

To: "Deepdale"

13 Pensioner Guard Huts

Wroth's Store + P.O.
Drummond's Steam Mill

Toodyay Brook

Toodyay Ford

OLD TOODYAY (1836-1860)

"Delamere"

Newcastle Bridge

AVON

To: Perth

Donegan's Cottage
Aboriginal Cemetery (1860's).
Gazetted 1916 First noted as an ancient burial ground in 1891.
Rev. Harper's home
C. Monger's Store + P.O.
Convict Depot: P.O. + School Residency
Anglican Church
Connor's Store
Freemasons Hotel
Wood's Store
Demasson's Store
Mechanics Institute
Newcastle Hotel and Mill
Newcastle RC Church + Cemetery (1864)

Mt. Anderson

NEWCASTLE (1860-1910) THEN RENAMED AS TOODYAY

RIVER

To: Perth

Nardee Cemetery

To: Northam

MAP 3

RESEARCH: Rica ERICKSON
MAP: John MASLIN

Toodyay and Newcastle.

8

be small independent farmers or employees, while many lonely men in distant huts could be shepherds employed by flockmasters.

In 1855 another Resident Magistrate of Toodyay went on a tour of inspection of the distant holdings of the Victoria Plains. He gave an account of several properties that shows how these shepherds were already rising in the social order from an employee to a prosperous pastoralist. Apart from the security of holding a pastoral lease, their social advancement was assisted by the transportation of convicts during the 1850s and 1860s. Convicts brought much needed labour to the colony and promoted the pastoralists' interests by creating markets for provisioning that were paid for by the British Government. [1]

Of equal importance was the number of skilled building tradesmen among the convicts as well as clerks and tutors. Homes built by the early colonists were necessarily simple. By 1832 about fifty-nine building tradesmen had come to the colony. The Census for that year listed two master builders, seventeen carpenters, twelve sawyers, eight brickmakers, three stonemasons, three lime burners, one wood turner, one thatcher and one glazier. A few years later when the colony seemed doomed to fail many of these tradesmen readily accepted offers of free passages to Sydney where more work was available. By 1837 only fourteen carpenters, three sawyers and two stonemasons remained. The two master builders moved to farming and pastoral activities on their grants.

Pioneers of the Avon and Toodyay districts were their own builders. On arrival at their grants they hastily erected wattle and daub huts, which if carefully built could last for years. They then began work on a more sturdy home with the help of employees. Stones were carried from the riverbank and mud was used for mortar since lime carted to their region was too expensive. They soon learnt that yellow clay was inferior to red clay while blue-grey clay was highly prized. Timber was rough-hewn from trees nearby while a blacksmith made the nails. Bulrushes or green 'blackboy' (Xanthorrhoea preissii – grass tree) tops were used for thatching. Glass windows were too costly so shutters were used instead. Dirt floors were common, but a few were paved with flat stones that were found on some hillsides. The chimney was usually built at one end, serving only one room, possibly to keep the other room cool in the hot summer months.

The wattle and daub huts became servants' quarters to be replaced later by more substantial cottages with walls of rammed earth or mud bricks

----

[1]   See Appendix 1.

(known as bats). These bricks took some time to assemble. Sometimes the wife of a small farmer made the 'bats'. She also became adept at plastering the inside walls, 'touching them up' during the annual spring clean. The outer walls could be made waterproof by the application of a liquid made of cow dung (a system widely used in India). The chimney was located at one end, made of stone or fired bricks. The doors of both rooms opened out to a lean-to or skillion which served as a verandah. Rooms could be added in line with the rest. The thatched roof, if well done, could last for fifty years or more and by the end of the century was usually replaced with galvanized iron.

After convicts were introduced in 1850 the warders' cottages were built of fired bricks to the same plan of two rooms but were distinguished by the chimney that was built centrally between them. After 1850 many pastoralists replaced their simple cottages by more spacious dwellings, the most popular being of two storeys, such as those built at Buckland and Bardeen. The builders were ticket-of-leave or expiree tradesmen. Plans were readily available in builders' journals. An enterprising bricklayer or brickmaker could become a building contractor.

The materials used in these buildings were more sophisticated than those used in the pioneering years. Bricks were fired in kilns, and lime was carted to mix with sand for mortar. Timbers were pit-sawn from forests along the road to Guildford and shingles were used instead of thatching. A law was passed in the 1850s banning thatch on all new buildings because of the risk of fire, but this was not always observed especially when mud brick homes were built. An expiree thatcher named Thomas Fothergill plied his trade at Toodyay for many years.

Although flat sheets of roofing iron had been advertised as early as November 1847 it was not readily accepted, being very costly. Wood for shingles could be easily obtained in the forest and such roofs were warmer in winter and cooler in summer. Marble mantelpieces and tiles for fireplaces were imported more commonly after 1850.

After the gold discoveries in the 1890s thousands of people had to be housed in short time. Galvanised iron became popular because it was light, weatherproof and easily erected by any handy man. On the goldfields it was used to roof the miners' camps built of hessian-covered timber frames, but some used galvanized iron for the walls. Prefabricated houses were also imported from America. In Perth and Fremantle as well as the goldfields whole suburbs of weatherboard houses were erected at modest prices. They also appeared in the country on newly settled farms.

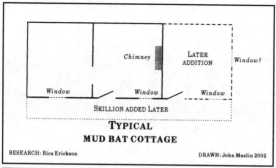

TYPICAL
MUD BAT COTTAGE

RESEARCH: Rica Erickson   DRAWN: John Maslin 2002

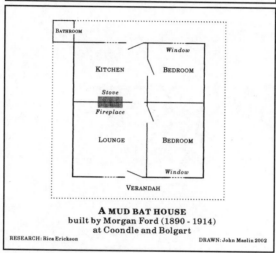

A MUD BAT HOUSE
built by Morgan Ford (1890 - 1914)
at Coondle and Bolgart

RESEARCH: Rica Erickson   DRAWN: John Maslin 2002

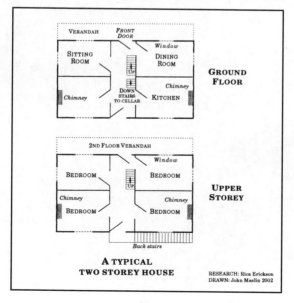

A TYPICAL
TWO STOREY HOUSE

RESEARCH: Rica Erickson
DRAWN: John Maslin 2002

11

Stone and mud wall, pre 1850 and a wall of dressed stone and lime mortar.
Courtesy Masters family.

Mud brick cottage built by Pritchard and Beard on a shared boundary. Courtesy Helen Henderson.

A thatched cottage built by Gavin at Solomon's Well. Photograph c.1900. Note the outdoor oven and water barrel.

Hasell's cottage built in c.1850s of kiln-fired brick and dressed stone.

Shingles were used by monks at New Norcia on cottages built for Aboriginal families, 1875. Benedictine Community of New Norcia Photographic collection, 73688P.

'Long Hill' cottage built in c.1860s in ruins showing how roofing changed over the years using sapling beams for thatch then dressed timber for galvanised iron roof. The brick chimney indicates cooking was done indoors. Courtesy Leo Camerer.

Buckland's two-storey house was added to the original 1840s cottage to the extreme right.

'Foggarthorpe'. A handsome home of the goldfields' period. The original Mt Anderson house to the right. Courtesy Shire of Toodyay.

A goldfields' type of house moved to a farm in 1921.

Sawmillers who had been turning out sleepers for railways decided to add houses to their catalogues. These were packaged for assembly, complete with galvanised iron chimneys and roofs, windows and doorframes and, if so desired, galvanised iron tanks.

The second and third generation of pastoralists built more extravagant homes planned by architects. The editor of the *Northam Advertiser* in May 1898 commented upon Toodyay's 'imposing and substantial buildings of ornate design and quite picturesque....the few and scattered homesteads of the past years for the most part superseded by handsome buildings.'

In the early days, many of these old homesteads functioned as centres for the community before shops, schools and churches were built in the nearby towns. Later generations of pastoralists were relieved of these responsibilities.

Railways built during the last years of the 1800s were also overcoming the isolation of distant homesteads. The colony was entering the age of machines. The social barriers of the past were crumbling when thousands of people came from overseas attracted by the gold discoveries. A man of doubtful origins could easily shed the stigma of the past in these new towns.

The twentieth century brought new methods of building and new building materials such as asbestos sheeting, fibreboard, cement and iron rafters. Housing problems could be solved by transportable houses or even caravans. Since very few old homes and early grants remain in the hands of descendants of the pioneers it is fitting that the stories of the old homesteads and communities be recorded. The Toodyay district is now a museum of heritage buildings.

References

G.F. Moore, *Diary of Ten Years' Eventful Life of an Early Settler in Western Australia,* London Edition, 1884. Facsimile edition UWA Press, Nedlands 1978.

Donald S. Garden, *Northam, an Avon Valley History,* Oxford University Press, Melbourne, 1979.

Margaret Pitt Morison and John White, eds., *Western Towns and Buildings*, UWA Press, Nedlands, 1979.

The following publications by Rica Erickson have been used extensively without specific references throughout the text of *Toodyay Homesteads: Past and Present.*

Rica Erickson, *The Drummonds of Hawthornden*, Lamb Paterson Pty Ltd, Osborne Park, 1969.

Rica Erickson, *The Victoria Plains*, Lamb Paterson Pty Ltd, Osborne Park, 1971.

Rica Erickson, *Old Toodyay and Newcastle*, Toodyay Shire Council, 1974.

Rica Erickson, *The Dempsters*, UWA Press, 1978.

Rica Erickson, *The Brand on His Coat*, UWA Press, Nedlands, 1983.

Rica Erickson, *The Bride Ships*, Hesperian Press, Carlisle, 1992.

2. OLD TOODYAY TOWN

In 1836 land was set aside for the proposed town of Toodyay. Boundaries were surveyed in the following year and included a ford across the Avon River, the only reliable crossing for many miles. Before long, all traffic moving between the Swan Valley and the Victoria Plains crossed the river at the Toodyay ford.

By the early 1840s all the large grants of land in the district were occupied. Around each homestead was a cluster of workmen's huts, while the shepherds lived on outstations as far away as the Victoria Plains and Moore River. However at the Toodyay townsite there were only two habitations. The first of these were the Police Barracks and stables built in 1842 where the policeman and his associate the Mounted Native Police were housed. The Barracks were located on the bank of the Avon River a short distance up from the ford, on a large grassy flat. It resembled a labourer's modest two roomed mud bat cottage, having a thatched roof and a dirt floor. The only difference was the placing of the chimney between the two rooms instead of at one end. One of these rooms was used as a courtroom when the Resident Magistrate of the district required it. On the rare occasions when an arrest was made it served as a lockup although the only restraint would be handcuffs.

The second building at the Toodyay townsite was erected by Ed Conlin. He and John Davidson were two of the Victoria Plains shepherds who by 1844 were competing against their masters. In 1844 Ed Conlin bought five acres next to the Toodyay Police Barracks. He had use of a wash pool in the river and built a solid barn there to store his year's supplies such as flour, tea and sugar. There was some advantage in building so close to the Barracks which would give protection against theft.

When it became known that Conlin was formerly an American sailor he was denied the titles to the land. It was then used by John Davidson.

By 1843 the Swan River Colony was on the brink of collapsing during a world wide trade recession. However, early in 1845 when news came that sandalwood fetched a high price in Asia the future became brighter. Many labourers competed with their employers in a hurried exodus into distant parts to cut sandalwood. Others chose to become waggoners. These men carted wool and sandalwood down to Guildford and returned with the settlers' annual supplies of stores. Others came and went on horseback. Traffic over the Avon at the ford was busy.

By 1849 William Herbert, a bootmaker, was living in a cottage by the ford on the bank opposite the Police Barracks. His brother John, a waggoner, occupied a five acre block on the same side of the river as William on the outskirts of the townsite boundaries. Another waggoner, Alex Warren, chose a block beside John Herbert's. Not all town lots had been surveyed by 1849 so intending purchasers were warned to build well within their supposed boundaries.

In 1849 William Herbert was appointed as the postmaster of the district. Apart from being the postmaster he also conducted a wayside inn in his cottage to be named 'The Royal Oak'.

In 1849, the Avon River came down in high flood damaging William Herbert's premises. He left Toodyay and opened a business in Guildford as a bootmaker. His brother John took over William's licence of 'The Royal Oak' and handed over his work as a waggoner to a brother-in-law John Davis. He built larger premises on higher ground keeping the name 'The Royal Oak'. He would not have been pleased to see Alex Warren build next door and apply for a licence for another wayside inn named 'The Gum Tree'.

The postmaster's duties were then given to Michael Clarkson, one of the earliest settlers who by 1849 was making a meagre living by running a very small flock of sheep on his land on the north of the townsite.

The future of the colony was assured when convicts were sent to Western Australia in 1850 to relieve a desperate shortage of labour. The main Convict Establishment was at Fremantle under E. Y. W. Henderson as Comptroller General, with Hiring Depots established in Perth and Guildford where Lt. Du Cane of the Royal Engineers was in charge. By then, Guildford was a thriving business centre and the addition of a Hiring Depot gave it added importance.

In 1851, Henderson agreed to open two more Convict Hiring Depots, at York and Toodyay and instructed Lt. Du Cane to send a contingent of ticket-of-leave to Toodyay.

The decision was made hastily. The site for the Toodyay Hiring Depot was made on the recommendation of the Resident Magistrate J. S. Harris. It was on the same side of the river as the Police Barracks, a forty-five and a half acre block opposite Mt Anderson and two miles up the Avon River from the ford. It was an isolated farmlet owned by a newcomer named Thomas Harrington who had planted 25 acres of wheat and barley and kept seventeen pigs. There was no road to Harrington's

17

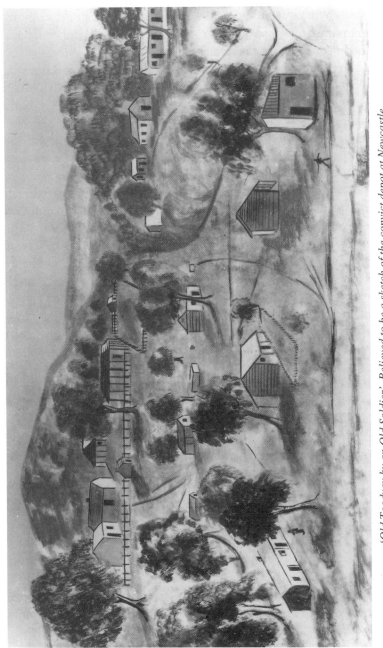

'Old Toodyay by an Old Soldier'. Believed to be a sketch of the convict depot at Newcastle. Courtesy of the Royal Western Australian Historical Society.

land. He crossed the river along a section that was usually dry and sandy for several months of the year.

The first contingent of forty ticket-of-leave men set out from Guildford in August 1851 with their stores, tents and bedding in two heavily laden wagons. Michael Clarkson who was appointed as the Superintendent of the proposed Convict Hiring Depot escorted them to Toodyay.

By the time they reached Toodyay rain was falling. The men had to cross the Avon to reach their destination and the Avon was beginning to flood. Without the assistance of several settlers the convicts would not have made the crossing. A large marquee was erected, but it may be assumed that some of the men slept at Harrington's hut and shed.

Lt. Du Cane's Annual Reports for 1852 and 1853 give details of the buildings constructed at the Toodyay Hiring Depot. The list is lengthy. By the end of 1852 a lock up had been built, roofed and weatherboarded and the gaoler's cottage commenced. A hut for a hospital had not been shingled for lack of shingle nails, but this was not of primary importance because only one man was sick enough to be placed there. Most important was the building of a commissariat store and the erection of a two-roomed house for two sappers. This was built, like the others, of mud bricks since the soil at Toodyay was not suitable for kiln-fired brickmaking.

However, progress on the buildings was impeded by the need to make a better road to the ford and townsite as well as a good route to shorten the way to Guildford. Also, the settlers' demands for ticket-of-leave labourers depleted Du Cane's workforce. At first there were twenty to sixty ticket-of-leave men at the Toodyay Hiring Depot but eighty were required by 1853, many of them set to work at road camps or hired out to settlers.

In 1851, the first of thirteen Pensioner Guards arrived with their families. Their duties were to act as warders. They lived in hastily erected straw huts at the Toodyay townsite. These huts were thatched to the ground with a stone chimney at one end and a doorway at the other. They were erected on allotments of land granted to them along the riverside on the opposite bank to the Toodyay Police Barracks.

The population at the townsite was increasing and because the policemen at the Barracks were often away patrolling their very large district extending from Northam to the Moore River, there was an obvious need for a permanent officer to be stationed in the townsite. A gaol and police quarters for the Colonial police were built at Toodyay nearer the inns. One of the Pensioner Guards, John Jones, was appointed as the warder and given £15 to build his cottage on Lot P3 on the northern part of the townsite. This gaol was in use by March 1853 when Reverend Wollaston wrote that it resembled the Albany Convict Gaol with twelve cells. The small village of Toodyay was growing in status.

Another Pensioner Guard who was a scholar opened a school in his straw hut where he taught some of the settlers' children.

In 1854 a large number of settlers met at 'The Royal Oak' which had become a centre for many of their activities, to form the Toodyay, Northam and Victoria Plains Agricultural Society. The Society then presented a petition to the Governor saying they had no church, no courthouse, no doctor, no bridges and no roads.

Funds were raised to qualify for a grant for a school that was large enough to accommodate the teacher's family. On Sundays the school was used for divine service by the Anglicans. Several grants of land had already been made for ecclesiastical purposes. One of these grants was favoured by Reverend Harper but it was located near the Hiring Depot some distance away from the townsite. His official duties required him to hold daily prayer meetings there as well as a full service on Sundays however the settlers preferred to have the church and school in town.

In 1856, when the new school was opened with much ceremony, the Catholics in the community began planning the building of a chapel at Toodyay. Their inspiration was Father Martelli the newly appointed parish priest. They had no dwelling for Martelli so he lived for a brief period in one of the two-roomed brick cottages already being built at the Depot. After that he occupied one of the straw huts when it was vacated. Later he moved to a wooden building near the Police Barracks which was large enough for him to hold divine service. The chapel at the townsite was consecrated in 1858.

The transfer of the Pensioner Guards from the straw huts to the brick cottages at the distant depot was made slowly. Some cottages were ready by 1856 after which their straw huts became temporary quarters for free immigrants waiting for employment. As a result the population at the town was not diminished by the departure of the Pensioner Guards. The Guards were able to claim small grants of land around the Depot which became known as the Pensioners Village.

In 1857, the settlers were dismayed when the British Government proposed to cease sending more convicts. The Hiring Depot was closed and one of the warders was retained as a caretaker. Nevertheless the town of Toodyay was growing steadily and surveyors were sent in 1859 to survey yet more allotments. But another flood in that year prevented work.

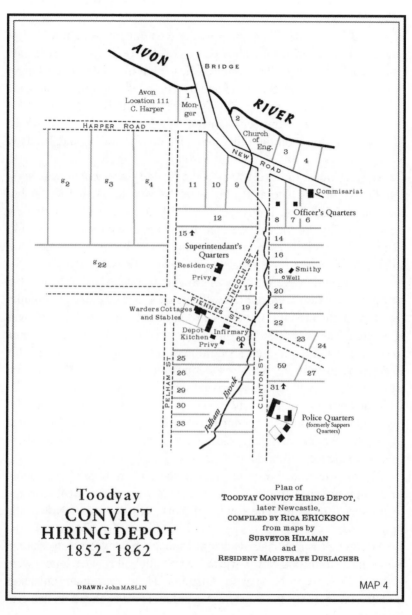

Toodyay
CONVICT
HIRING DEPOT
1852 - 1862

Plan of
TOODYAY CONVICT HIRING DEPOT,
later Newcastle,
COMPILED BY RICA ERICKSON
from maps by
SURVEYOR HILLMAN
and
RESIDENT MAGISTRATE DURLACHER

DRAWN: John MASLIN

MAP 4

Toodyay Convict Depot.
Site becomes Newcastle, 1860.

Having been flooded on several occasions in the past the government decided to abandon the Toodyay townsite. Surveyors were sent in 1860 to survey 300 acres for a new town around the Pensioners Village to be named Newcastle. Some enterprising men quickly bought town lots and built hotels and stores. The licences of the Toodyay inns were then cancelled. Settlers travelled to Newcastle to patronise the new and bigger hotels and to buy from the stores and bakery. These facilities soon made Newcastle a bustling town, while Toodyay lost its identity. In 1861 a bridge was built by contract labour at Newcastle for the convenience of those who lived on the other side of the river and up the Toodyay Valley.

Another flood in 1862 washed the bridge away but it was soon rebuilt by convict labour. Buildings at Newcastle did not suffer but the foundations of the Toodyay school, although on high ground, were undermined by the torrent of water that swept down the hill behind it. With the loss of this last community amenity at Toodyay, the old town soon faded away. In time it was to be known as West Toodyay.

In the meantime Newcastle was growing fast. During 1864 and 1865 new police quarters were built as well as a gaol. The Catholic community and the Anglicans built churches in the new town and a doctor was appointed. The new Resident Magistrate used one of the Depot Stores as his office and requested the addition of several rooms to make it his Residency. In time, the children's education was supplied by several women in town who taught at private schools in their homes.

Transportation of convicts ceased in 1868 by which time several expirees were well-to-do members of the district. They were admitted to societies which previously rejected them and were accepted as office bearers in the Road Board and Town Council.

Western Australia always regarded as the Cinderella colony suddenly rose to prominence in the 1890s when many thousands of men came to prospect for gold. The towns of York, Northam and Newcastle flourished.

After the prospectors arrived confusion arose between Newcastle in Western Australia and Newcastle in New South Wales when letters were addressed simply to Newcastle, Australia. There were many mistakes in delivery. In 1910, the Western Australian town changed its name to Toodyay.

References:

Rica Erickson, *Old Toodyay and Newcastle,* Toodyay Shire Council, 1974.

Alexandra Hasluck, *Royal Engineer*, Angus and Robertson, 1973. Quoting from Parliamentary Papers on Convict Discipline and Transportation 1849-65, Vol. VI, Report of DuCane, July 1852 and Appendix E 31/12/1853.

A. R. Pashley, *Policing Our State*, Educant, Cloverdale, WA, 2000

Government Gazette, 6 May, 1910.

Records in the State Library concerning land titles, maps, and Resident Magistrates' letters.

3. MORBY COTTAGE

'Morby Cottage' at Northam was built in 1836 by John Morrell who arrived in the Swan River Colony in 1831 with a large family. He was a builder by trade and expected to make a good living. The building materials he brought with him qualified him for a large grant of land (Avon Location P1) which he selected near the proposed townsite of Northam. His cargo included panelled doors, window frames, glass, slates for roofing, locks, hinges, putty, paint and seven hundred weight of nails. Since he expected to build elegant homes he included black and plain marble and statuary chimney pieces.

'Morby Cottage'.
Photograph: Robyn Taylor 2004.

'Morby Cottage'. Back verandah
showing stone and mortar construction.
Photograph: Robyn Taylor 2002.

Morrell spent five years in Perth before moving to 'Morby'. During this time the Swan River Colony had been on the brink of collapse as a result of reports in England of poor soil and harsh conditions. Many colonists had left for Eastern Australia, but Morrell like others had sunk all their capital in the colony and could not abandon their investment in Crown land. While in Perth he had leased his Northam grant to Peter and William Chidlow who made the improvements required to secure Morrell's title to the land. They cleared trees, ploughed some ground and ran a dairy herd. They made butter which was salted down in casks for sale at Perth. The Chidlow brothers received 1450 acres as payment from Morrell and then teamed up with William Jones to make the improvements on an adjacent grant known as 'Katrine' owned by the widow of Dr J. P. Lyttleton.

When John Morrell moved to his Avon Valley grant in 1836 he built the most comfortable home in all the area 'over the hills' along the Avon River. It was well built of stone and mud, of generous proportions with the refinement of glass windows, the first along the Valley.

The Morrell family owned a large flock of sheep. Each year before shearing they were washed at a pool in the Avon River. In October 1843 when a workman slipped into deep water he was saved from drowning by John Morrell, who died a few days later of a chill. His son Frederick, at the age of twenty-three years then managed the family affairs.

'Morby' was halfway between York and Toodyay. During 1849 to 1853 the settlers in the Northam area went to 'Morby' to collect the weekly mail. Apart from serving as a post office the dining room at 'Morby' was used regularly by the Resident Magistrate as a courthouse until in 1866 a courthouse was built at Northam townsite. A small village was growing there. Community affairs which were formerly held at 'Morby' moved to the town instead. When the Northam Roads Board was created in 1871 Frederick Morrell retired to live in town.

Frederick Morrell served the community very well for many years until his death in 1899. The property was divided and by 1914 only a few acres around 'Morby' were still in family hands. His unmarried daughter ran a small dairy there until she died in 1920.

'Morby' cottage was eventually bought by the Northam Town Council and restored using a heritage grant from the National Estate Programme. Restoration was completed in 1988 and the cottage was opened to the public as a museum. The cottage had been in relatively good condition unlike other houses built before the convict period. The front walls were coated with cement but the back walls remain as John Morrell built them – an example of his skill as a builder.

References

G.F. Moore, *Diary of Ten Years' Eventful Life of an Early Settler in Western Australia,* · London Edition, 1884. Facsimile edition UWA Press, Nedlands 1978.

Donald S. Garden, *Northam, an Avon Valley History*, Oxford University Press, Melbourne, 1979.

4. NEWLEYINE

'Newleyine' (Avon Location e) was granted to William Heal (1782-1845) formerly a tallow chandler. He and his sister Martha (1794-1861) came to the colony in the *Minstrell* in 1830, accompanied by the families of their brother Charles and their sister Mary Ann Morgan. Mary Ann's husband died in 1830 and Charles died in 1831. The two widows remained in the Swan district while William and Martha occupied their grant at Beverley. In 1836 they were given permission to relocate their land near Morrell's.

In June that year when G.F. Moore was exploring east of Northam he visited 'Newleyine' and wrote, 'It is gratifying to see the progress which five weeks industry has enabled him to make. Several acres of wheat already in the ground, a considerable [kitchen] garden, two huts for present residence, the side walls of a substantial house, a stockyard and sheep pen all attest to his labour and assiduity.'

Heal and his labourer John Danks were assisted by a young nephew Charles Heal and two lads named George Agett and Frederick Purkis whose fathers owned adjacent grants which Heal was to acquire, partly because he performed the location duties on their land.

On Heal's eastern boundary were two 1000-acre grants which he had selected for his relatives the Morgan family. Location T1 was for nephew Abraham and T2 for Mary Ann. She had married John Taylor Cooke in 1836 who made a precarious living as a carpenter in the Swan district. Cooke then leased 'Katrine' which was only a short distance down the Avon River from 'Newleyine'.

Abraham Morgan and his mother became neighbours when he built a mud brick cottage on his grant T1 which he named 'Bardeen'.

William Heal died in 1845 bequeathing 'Newleyine' to his two sisters, Martha Heal and widow Morgan. In 1847 Martha retired to Fremantle leaving 'Newleyine' in charge of John Taylor Cooke and his wife whose lease of 'Katrine' had expired. Mrs Cooke and her brother Abraham Morgan would inherit 'Newleyine' after Martha Heal's death. It was advantageous for Mary Ann and Abraham to exchange their grants T1 and T2 to bring her two properties together. The deeds were not signed until 1851 but Cooke could have been looking over the future possibilities. There was no water on Location T2. The nearest was at Gabbigen Spring. That was claimed by Major Nairn who said it was on

McDermott's grant Location U which he was leasing apparently with the option of purchase.

Cooke suspected the spring was outside Location U, and applied to buy a small freehold block around it. After years of delay the boundaries of the surrounding grants were surveyed in 1849 and Nairn had to admit he had no claim to the Spring.

Cooke built a new house at 'Newleyine' that year, engraving the date 1849 over the door. He and Mary took up residence, using their first home as servants' quarters. Cooke built a steam mill and enlarged the area under crop and began fencing the boundaries of his land to keep out trespassing stock, to the annoyance of travellers who were denied the use of a well-worn track through his property.

John Taylor Cooke was a founding member of the Toodyay, Northam and Victoria Plains Agricultural Society in 1856 and won prizes for his rams. His son Nathaniel took his place in 1857.

In 1857 Nathaniel Cooke leased large areas of land in the Champion Bay district and was to establish a thriving property at 'Arrino'. His brother Henry John became the mainstay at 'Newleyine'. The two brothers married in 1863.

John Taylor Cooke died in 1875 at the age of 67 years. His wife Mary Ann died in 1886 at seventy-two years. Their son, Henry John and his wife Jane had thirteen children though several died young. Six were married. Henry Merino, their son who inherited 'Newleyine' was married in 1890 to Fanny Phillips of 'Culham'. She was thirteen years older than him but a very handsome woman. Her mother strongly opposed the union partly because at the time of his marriage he was only twenty-five years old and known already to be a heavy drinker. During one of his drunken bouts he took pleasure in shooting the portrait of his mother-in-law. Henry and Fanny had no children and after his death in 1902 'Newleyine' was leased. A few years later R.H. Middleton and Lionel Viveash bought 'Newleyine'. They were related by marriage, since Middleton had married Lionel's sister. Middleton who owned the section which included the 'Newleyine' homestead had a large family of daughters. In their old age they remembered the homes at 'Newleyine' and sketched plans of both. They also remembered two Chinese gardeners who leased a small plot of ground near the older house where they grew vegetables which they peddled around the streets of Northam. When the spring dried up about 1935 the Chinese moved elsewhere.

After World War II 'Newleyine' was sold to Samuel Viveash. He demolished the house which Cooke built and used the bricks to build a home out of sight of the road. The ruins of Heal's cottage became hidden by a large pepper tree. Close by are the graves of William and Martha Heal. Their old home is remembered as a two-storey rectangular building with an attic and a steeply pitched roof.

References

G.F. Moore, *Diary of Ten Years' Eventful Life of an Early Settler in Western Australia,* London Edition, 1884. Facsimile edition UWA Press, Nedlands 1978.

P.W.H. Theil, *Twentieth Century Impressions of Western Australia,* 1901. Reprinted Hepsrian Press, Carlisle, 2000.

Yvonne and Kevin Coates, *Lonely Graves of Western Australia and Burials at Sea,* Hesperian Press, Carlisle, 1986.

Mary Bentley, *The Morgan Family* 1750-1986. Privately published.

(Bentley's references include two volumes in which are complete diaries, farm journals, official documents regarding land holdings, maps, reminiscences, memorabilia. Permission to use this material has been generously given by descendants.)

5. BARDEEN

'Bardeen' (Avon Location T1 of 1000 acres) was occupied around 1840 by Abraham Morgan and his mother. They lived in a cottage called the River House that had been constructed near the Avon River. Around 1844 Abraham built another cottage on the location when he married Annie Morrell. They were to have three children. Their only son William John was born at the River House in 1845. A daughter Susanna was born in 1852. The two cottages were built of stone and mud. The floors were paved with flat stones and the roofs were thatched. Old Mrs Morgan passed away in 1853.

'Bardeen', c.1870s.
Painter unknown.
Courtesy Morgan family.

In 1857, several years after convicts were brought to the colony, Abraham Morgan employed an expiree brick maker named John Bonsor to fire some bricks at a new site for the building of a fine two-storey house. Their third child Mary Ann was born there in 1861.

Until the family moved into this new home their young son William John helped his mother at the second cottage bringing wood and water. By 1852 he was helping his father by driving a horse around the threshing floor. At eleven years he was working with the men who were seeding

29

and harvesting. At twelve years of age he was shearing lambs and at thirteen years was driving a horse and harrows to cover the newly sown wheat. At fourteen he ploughed a field with a single furrow plough and was also a good reaper with the scythe. At fifteen he got in the harvest and helped to treat 1000 scabby sheep with a dressing of tobacco water at the rate of a bottle for each affected sheep. At sixteen he was feeding sheaves of wheat into a threshing machine. He could do everything required on the farm including sowing wheat by hand from a box slung around his neck. He could kill and dress a sheep and had mastered every skill required by a farmer and pastoralist.

Between seasons William John Morgan attended a small school at 'Newleyine', then at fifteen years he studied at Bishops College in Perth for a year. Between terms he had work at 'Bardeen'. He also helped to cart wool and sandalwood to Guildford.

The 'River House' was subsequently occupied by Morgan's employees. Improvements were made to the cottage by replacing the original walls with fired brick. John Bonsor's descendants say that the bricks were laid around the old walls and after that job was completed the original walls were dismantled and handed out through the doors and windows piece-by-piece.

William John began further renovations to the 'River House' in 1870, possibly because he was contemplating marriage to Mary Jane Connolly. It was replastered and painted, timber floors were put in, and glass bought for windows. However, the death of his father Abraham Morgan in 1871, at the early age of 51 years, put a temporary halt to William John's plans. Apparently it was agreed the young couple would move into the parents' two-storey house, while the mother and sister would occupy the 'River House'. Before his marriage he undertook improvements to the farm and the two-storey house.

In 1872 William John hired John Bonsor and his son to make kiln-fired bricks. These required great loads of timber to be fetched. Also an expert stonemason named Peter Brehart, an expiree, began work sinking wells and building a large granary before starting work on the two-storey house, adding a long wing of rooms and a back verandah.

The marriage of William John Morgan to Mary Jane Connolly was celebrated in 1873. They reared eight of their ten children. He became active in public affairs and in 1881 he was elected to the Northam Road Board and served on it for twenty-one years. He was a founding member of the Northam Agricultural Society and was a member of the Northam Race Club.

In 1882 W. J. Morgan and his neighbour J. T. McDermott sent 700 sheep and seven horses to a pastoral lease on the Lennard River in the Kimberley district which was opened up for settlement soon after Alexander Forrest explored the region in 1879. Misfortune hit when the river came down in flood in 1885 and the whole flock was drowned.

By 1885 William John Morgan was well established at 'Bardeen' having acquired several old grants and extended his pastoral leases beyond Northam. In his old age he recorded his memories, and when he died in June 1924 he left a legacy of family papers that a granddaughter used in 1986 to compile a complete record.

'Bardeen' is one of the few early grants to remain in family hands by the year 2004.

References
Mary Bentley (nee Morgan), 'The Morgan Family 1750-1986'. Privately published.
Interviews with descendants of some employees, chiefly the Bonsor family.

6. EGOLINE AND BAYLIE FARM

'Egoline' and 'Baylie Farm' (on the opposite bank of the Avon River from 'Bardeen') were allotted to Charles Dawson Ridley (1787-1845) and Charles Ridley Hinds (born 1811/12). They came to the Swan River Colony together on the *Wanstead* in 1830. Ridley's family arrived soon afterwards while Hinds' father Richard Hinds (1781-1843) arrived in 1837 with another member of the family named Richard Brinsley Hinds. Obviously the two families were related. Both claimed grants at Guildford and in the Avon districts.

Charles Dawson Ridley received Avon location Z (8750 acres) to be known as 'Baylie Farm' while Charles Ridley Hinds received adjacent grants Locations 17, 61, 62 (4463 acres) named 'Egoline'. The two families settled on their farms at Guildford and apparently engaged someone else to occupy and make improvements on their Avon Valley grants. Stone and mud cottages were built on both. Lack of building experience is evident. A room in one cottage was a foot wider at one end than the other with protruding stones. In time these were hidden by several coatings of mud plaster, encouraging the thought that mud bricks were used.

Charles Dawson Ridley died in 1845 and his son Charles was drowned in 1848. Lewis Ridley then managed their Guildford farm while his brother Joseph preferred to continue his career as a policeman in the Toodyay district.

The Hinds family also suffered bereavements. Richard Hinds Sr died in 1843 and his son Richard died in 1846. Mrs Hinds remained on the Guildford farm but her son Charles decided to begin afresh in Tasmania. When he advertised 'Egoline' for sale or lease the two Ridley brothers decided to include 'Baylie Farm' in the auction held in April 1848.

'Egoline' was quoted as a well-developed property with a suitable dwelling and outbuildings, with a well-trenched garden beside the spring, fruit trees and two acres of vineyard. Fifty acres were fenced and under cultivation. The grant was already mortgaged to Edward Hamersley who was living in France. Robert de Burgh leased 'Egoline' for a year after which John Sewell leased it in 1850 with the option of purchase. Sewell already had a flock of sheep grazing at 'Egoline' after the floods of 1847 resulted in plenty of feed along the Avon River. 'Baylie Farm' was leased to John Thomas Smith who had been working on the grant.

'Egoline'.
Photograph: Robyn Taylor
2002.

'Egoline' verandah.
Photograph: Robyn Taylor
2002.

'Egoline', c.1900.
Courtesy Randle family.

The parlour, c.1900.
Courtesy Randle family.

In 1850 a bushfire threatened the house at 'Egoline' and burnt the vineyard shortly before Sewell and his large family moved in. Members of the Sewell family had been in the colony since 1842. Two of the elder sons had preceded the rest of the family's arrival and were sharefarming in the Avon Valley. In 1850 another son Sampson married Elizabeth Yule and moved to 'Oakabella' in the Geraldton district. The youngest son Frederick remained at 'Egoline' to help his father.

The Smiths at 'Baylie Farm' had an equally large family. Their twelfth child was born in 1874 shortly before Christmas. Within a few days John Thomas Smith, his wife and three of their children died. The twenty-year-old son Richard then shouldered the responsibility of rearing the remaining children, a duty he fulfilled for twenty years.

As a young boy he was in charge of his brothers and sisters as they walked to the Katrine school. When the Avon was running high over the ford he would test the depth of water before taking them 'pickaback' across the River. One of his schoolmates was Marie Wilkerson who later became the teacher at 'Katrine' and taught the youngest of the Smiths.

Richard Smith married her when he was forty and she was thirty one. The ceremony was conducted at St Saviours Church at 'Katrine'. As an old man he remembered watching the convict parties at work building the ford at 'Katrine'. Stones were skidded down the steep slopes of Noondenning Hill and then carried to be carefully assembled at the ford. The cracks between were filled with heavy blue clay which they crushed and puddled by stamping on it with their boots on and their trousers rolled up.

In the convict years the 'Katrine' ford was known as 'Mrs Slade's Crossing'. After an unprecedented flood in 1862 stakes were driven in beside the ford to guide travellers. After that the Northam Road Board assumed responsibility for maintaining the ford.

The Smiths remained at 'Baylie Farm' until near the turn of the century. Richard Smith retired to Northam and died in 1931. The stories he told of the old days were treasured by James Masters whose parents bought 'Glen Avon' in 1901 and, like Richard Smith, regularly attended services at the Katrine Church.

References

Donald S. Garden, *Northam, an Avon Valley History*, Oxford University Press, Melbourne, 1979.

William and Margaret de Burgh, *The Breakaways*, St George Books, Perth, 1981.

J.R. Masters unpublished notes by kind permission of his family.

7. HAMPTON FARM

'Hampton Farm' was originally part of William Heal's property and was bought in 1855 by two brothers Joseph Lockyer (1817-1912) and Thomas Lockyer (1820-1880). Both men had worked previously for Charles Pratt who owned a grant at Beverley and another at 'Buckland' in the Northam district. After Pratt's son-in-law J.M. Dempster left 'Buckland' in 1848 to lease Rottnest the Lockyer brothers leased 'Oakfield', a grant that was located next to 'Egoline'.

Joseph was a noted amateur jockey and racehorse owner. He won the Queens Plate twice and appeared also in most race meetings, riding winners until he was over 60 years old. The Lockyers' father was a millwright and they learnt the trade from him. When the brothers bought another property known as 'Hampton Farm' they built a horse-powered mill there. It survived several floods including one in 1862 when the waters of the Avon River came lapping around the foundations.

In 1859 Joseph married Lydia Simmons who came to the colony in 1841 as a lady companion to Mrs Francisco, the wife of a wealthy man. Lydia often reminded her six children of this prestigious arrival.

Joseph became the sole owner of 'Hampton Farm' in 1864 which in time he enlarged to 3000 acres and developed with the help of several ticket-of-leave men until 1880. At the time of the gold rush during 1890-1910 he delivered the mails to the Yilgarn leaving the management of Hampton Farm to his two sons.

After Joseph Lockyer's death in 1912 his sons and a daughter inherited different parts of 'Hampton Farm'. The son Albert sold his part around 1919 to F. A. Hill who changed the name to 'Hampton Vineyard'.

References
Donald S. Garden, *Northam, an Avon Valley History,* Oxford University Press, Melbourne, 1979.

Battye Library. Dempster papers. Acc. 971A, 677A and 1186A.

MSS in the hands of Mary Hargreaves and other descendants, copies in the hands of Rica Erickson.

Interviews with Mrs Patti Parkins, another descendant.

8. BUCKLAND

'Buckland' (Avon Location W of 7986 acres) was assigned in 1836 to Charles Pratt (1791-1853). He came to Fremantle in January 1830 in his own ship *Eagle*. One of his crew was James Maclean Dempster (1810-1890) who was given command of the ship until 1836 when it was sold.

Pratt qualified for two large grants, 'Addington' at Beverley and 'Buckland' near Northam, assigned to him in 1836. Two employees, the Lockyer brothers were sent to 'Buckland' to perform the location duties, which they did by building a cottage, clearing some land and planting fruit trees and a kitchen garden.

'Addington' was managed by James Maclean Dempster, who had married Ann Pratt in 1836. They moved to 'Buckland' after Pratt received the titles to that grant in February 1841.

Dempster enlarged the cottage as the number of his children increased. Sawn timbers and battens were carted from Guildford by the Hancock brothers, along with 1000 kiln-fired bricks and some building iron (possibly part of the consignment of flat sheets of galvanised iron imported in the late 1840s). The carpenters were Samuel Smith and James Welbourn. The Lockyer brothers then built a stone barn and a horse-drawn flourmill for Dempster.

Pratt was a difficult man to deal with. He had a serious disagreement with Dempster in 1848. Dempster then leased Rottnest and took his wife and seven children to live there. 'Buckland' was leased to George Chitty and Fred Lee until Pratt died in 1853. He bequeathed everything to his wife and after her death 'Buckland' was to be divided between his grandchildren Anne Ellen and Charles Edward. The remaining properties were divided among the others, the Beverley property going to the eldest grandson James Pratt. James Dempster and Anne Ellen received all the stock and machinery at 'Buckland', but paid her mother for the rental of the property.

They moved into 'Buckland' and built another cottage parallel to the first with an enclosed garden between them. The old cottage became the servants' quarters. The Dempster's family home was still somewhat crowded so the eldest daughter Annie and the youngest son William Simon spent some time at Guildford with their indulgent grandmother.

In the 1860s the other sons took up pastoral leases to the east of 'Buckland' and also at Esperance which Charles Edward and Andrew agreed to manage, taking it in turns to live there. They both married in 1867. Daughter Ann was already married in 1861 to T.H. Gull at Guildford, while in 1867 and 1868 Jane and Marion married the Hamersley brothers Edward and Hugh of 'Wilberforce' at York. The youngest son William Simon at the age of eighteen years was made manager at 'Buckland' under his father's direction. After Granny Pratt died in 1872 Captain Dempster decided to build extensions to the old home. His sons agreed to share the costs which he carefully recorded.

'Buckland' c. 1900, built 1876. Original 1840s cottage can be seen at the rear.

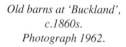

Old barns at 'Buckland', c.1860s. Photograph 1962.

For the next few years while the house was being built, the four brothers endeavoured to define where each would live. Early in 1874 they bought Drummond's Steam Mill and 'Vine Cottage' where Andrew and his family lived.

In February that year timber was carted from the saw millers and work was begun on building the new house at 'Buckland'. The contractors were John Richardson and Peter Brehart, both expirees. Brehart was a stonemason, reputed to be the first in the colony to use dynamite. He began work by sinking a stone well at 'Buckland' and then erected a large stone barn, before the timbers arrived for the homestead in February 1874. All the work was done by men of convict origin, excepting some who did the carting. The new 'Buckland' home was completed in time for a big housewarming party in August 1876 attended by 34 members of the family and some friends.

The sons had not settled their differences regarding who should live at 'Buckland'. Andrew decided to live at Esperance again, leaving William Edward to carry on at 'Vine Cottage'. William Simon refused to leave 'Buckland' and took his bride there in 1878. All were shocked when their mother died in August 1880 and their father married Fanny Shaw only four months later.

By 1886 James Pratt Dempster, the eldest son, was married and living at 'Addington' in the Beverley district. Andrew owned 'Muresk' and Charles Edwards had bought 'Springfield' near Northam. Captain Dempster and his second wife occupied a room in the upper storey at 'Buckland'. He died of a fall from the balcony in 1890. William Simon died two years later leaving his widow Maud to manage 'Buckland' assisted by her brother until he left for England.

Maud Dempster had a flair for breeding stock and was highly respected for the number of trophies she won at Agricultural Shows. Her son was educated in England and when he came of age in 1903 he took charge at 'Buckland' which was his inheritance. Maud then bought a neglected property at Grass Valley. After bringing it to productivity she gave it to her youngest son Cedric.

Frederick's wife found the house at 'Buckland' to be too large for their needs. She encouraged him to buy a large pastoral station in the Northwest. 'Buckland' was sold and the new owners lived in the ground floor. The two-storey section became very dilapidated. The property changed hands several times. One owner reorganised the rooms for use as a holiday and weekend resort. The next owner restored 'Buckland' to its original state and used it as a private residence. Subsequent owners were also aware of the historic value of the old home.

References
Rica Erickson, *The Dempsters,* UWA Press, Nedlands, 1978.

Dempster family papers in Battye Library 1728A and a very large collection of letters and papers in the hands of descendants which were graciously lent for copying and publication.

9. THE BUILDERS AT BUCKLAND AND OTHER HOMESTEADS.

The time taken to build 'Buckland' was comparable with that required for building of most homesteads in the Toodyay and Victoria Plains districts during 1850 to 1890. The farm records for 'Springhill', Benjamin Piggott's property near Australind are almost as large as Dempster's for 'Buckland'. They give further evidence of this time span and also support the claim that most of the building tradesmen in the colony were men of convict origin.

The sequence of work may be judged from a listing of jobs, their timing as shown in the wages books, and the journals and records of goods bought from the homestead stores.

The Dempsters placed orders for timber in 1873 with a timber milling company operated by John Challinor (convict number 6074) who employed several expirees at his mill at Jingalup on the road from Guildford to Toodyay. There were boards, rafters, battens, lattice, shingles and some beams as long as twenty-one feet. Two of the carters were colonials of early years, John Cook and Francis Hastings, who thereby cancelled debts to Dempster. The long beams were carted by Challinor's men. These timbers were brought as required during February 1874 to October 1876.

In April 1874 Peter Brehart (6521) having completed the stone granary barn and other farm buildings, signed the contract to begin work on the building of the homestead. In the same month John Bonsor (728) employed Charles Reilly (8117) to make 72,000 bricks, a work that continued until June 1875.

John Langham (7182) then began bricklaying. By October 1874 John Richardson (6089) a carpenter, employed other men to put the long beams in place. Sheoak shingles were carted in August 1875. After the roofing was finished, the work began in January and February of 1876 of carting the ceiling lathes, battens and lattice. John Richardson then left. (In 1882 he sailed to South Australia.) In March to June 1876 John Weasley (9605) joined the work force. He was a builder, bricklayer and mason. By May that year the flooring boards and rafters were carted.

The dominance of building tradesmen of convict origin in the district became apparent when records were studied of other pastoralists who employed ticket-of-leave men. (See Appendix 3)

10. KATRINE

'Katrine' (Avon Location T of 2560 acres) was granted to Dr J.P. Lyttleton who died at Albany in 1835 while on duty as a medical officer. His widow leased the Avon grant to Peter Chidlow and William Jones. While ploughing a small field they were killed by Aborigines. It is not known in what way the white men had offended. The attack was not expected because Hannapwirt was one of the party and had been on very friendly terms with Morrell and Heal as well as with G.F. Moore during his exploration of the area beyond Northam.

'Katrine'.
Photograph: Robyn Taylor
2003.

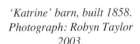
'Katrine' barn, built 1858.
Photograph: Robyn Taylor
2003.

Despite this attack by the Aborigines John Taylor Cooke, whose wife was Heal's niece, had no qualms about leasing 'Katrine' in 1838 for seven years. They lived in a modest cottage near the ford where travellers often sought accommodation. In 1842 Cooke secured a licence for a wayside inn there to be known as the 'Bush Inn'. He accepted the duties of postmaster when a weekly mail service from York to Toodyay was introduced.

When Dr S.W. Viveash bought 'Katrine' in 1842 he extended Cooke's lease to 1847. Then in 1848 Viveash sent James Wilkerson to manage the property. He was only seventeen years old so was paid half a man's wages, receiving rations as well. Wilkerson married Elizabeth Farmer in 1851. They had six children. Since she was colonial-born she was accustomed to a pioneering life. James enlarged the cottage and built a substantial granary of stone. Some of the labourers were ticket-of-leave men sent to him by Viveash between the years 1857 and 1875.

A notable feature of the barn was slots built high up the wall. These narrowed inwardly and then widened again into the interior. Similar narrowing slots were built in several colonial buildings. In modern times they have been explained erroneously as gun slots to help ward off marauding Aborigines. In fact they were specially designed for cooling. They worked on the principle that hot air when compressed becomes cooler. Spontaneous combustion in damp hay or grain is thus prevented. Similar slots are to be seen in several old buildings in the Avon districts. At 'Summer Hill' near New Norcia they are at floor level in the end walls of a dairy. They are at the end walls of an open stable at 'Irwin House' on the Greenough. Boers in South Africa also cooled their houses by narrowing slots in the walls, while in Arabia before air-conditioning units were invented, the homes of the wealthy had towers above with doors opening on to the four walls which could be adjusted to face the appropriate side when hot desert winds were blowing.

A small brick cottage was built at 'Katrine' at a discreet distance from that occupied by Wilkerson's family. This is said to have been built for Mary Viveash who went to 'Katrine' to keep house for her brothers Samuel and Simeon. They were sent to 'Katrine' for experience in management for the time they would take charge. Mary is thought to have planted the olive trees which shade the cemetery at St Saviours Church, built in 1861 on an acre of land given by Dr Viveash.

The church was built by John Sewell of 'Egoline' under contract to the building committee comprised of J. Wilkerson, J.T. Cooke and Abraham Morgan. Stone was quarried from Noondenning Hill and carried across the river by ticket-of-leave men and some Chinese coolies.

In 1864 a school was completed at a short distance from the homestead and church. An expiree clerk lived and taught there until 1871. After that whenever sufficient numbers of pupils could be mustered the school was reopened by a succession of women teachers.

By 1865 Samuel Viveash left 'Katrine' and joined with Charles Wilkerson and an elderly man named Thomas Middleton to take up a pastoral lease near Roebourne known as 'Indernoona'. Simeon Viveash was old enough to manage 'Katrine' so Wilkerson Sr leased a neighbouring grant named 'Glen Avon'. It had been badly flooded in 1862 so there was a lot of work to be done there.

In 1867 Simeon Viveash employed two ticket-of-leave men, John Greenhalgh a brickmaker and John Davis a sawyer, to assemble the materials for building a two-storey home at 'Katrine'. In 1870 he engaged Peter Brehart a stonemason and John Weasley a bricklayer to begin building. It was nearly completed in 1872 when a flood filled the cellar and damaged the foundations. Repairs were made with some urgency because Simeon's marriage to Mary Lukin was to take place in November that year. They had many children. Additions were joined to the rear of the house with an external staircase to facilitate the discreet entry of servants.

After Simeon's death in 1904 the property changed hands. By the 1990s the barn wall was in danger of collapsing. The new owner, R. Downie gradually moved the wall upright again in a simple year-long operation. The homestead was restored equally skilfully. Some outbuildings appropriate to the period were added and the complex was opened as a museum.

References

Diaries of Dr S.W. Viveash, Battye Library, WAA 1226A.
Employers of ticket-of-leave men, Battye Library, WABI file 3780 A.
Nancy E. Withnell Taylor, *Yeera-muk-a-doo*. Reprinted Hesperian Press, Carlisle, 1987.
Interviews with J.R. Masters for notes on the Katrine church with reminiscences of Richard Smith.
Interviews with R. and C.M. Downie.

11. GLEN AVON

'Glen Avon' (Location X of 5730 acres) was assigned originally to Hugh George Smith in 1833. He was disappointed to find it included rocky hills and made no attempt to occupy it. He drowned in the Swan River in 1842 and the land was bought by Lt. Frederick Slade the same year.

'Glen Avon' (side view).
1980s.

'Glen Avon' from the road.
The original cottage at
centre.
Courtesy Masters family.

Slade arrived in the colony in January 1840 on the *Westmoreland* with his wife and children and their governess Jane Nairn and his bachelor brother Henry Slade, as well as James Clinch a labourer. At first he leased Yule's grant at Guildford, known as 'Houghton', and remained there while searching for land to purchase. After deciding to buy Smith's Location X on the Avon he was impatient to occupy it. Mrs Slade chose the name of 'Glen Avon' for their land and while a cottage was being built by Clinch they lived in a small hut at 'Katrine'.

Frederick and Henry Slade intended establishing stud flocks. Henry sailed to Tasmania and bought 300 well-bred ewes, but due to bad weather could land only 60 at Fremantle. Undeterred he returned to Tasmania to buy more.

43

When the cottage at 'Glen Avon' was completed James Clinch was put to work building a substantial barn of stone and mud further up the slope. After losing so many sheep at sea Frederick Slade was more interested in cattle. He soon earned a reputation as one of the most successful pastoralists and farmers in the district. In 1846 he was appointed as a member of the Toodyay Road Committee. Then when Captain Scully of Bolgart returned to Ireland in 1847 Slade was appointed as Resident Magistrate in his stead.

Official business that year was demanding. He reported to the Colonial Secretary in Perth on the movement of 16,000 sheep from Toodyay to the Victoria Plains. Also he had to deal with conflicting claims for the right to cut sandalwood. He employed William Dodd (1804-1875) as his clerk. Dodd was accustomed to clerical work, having trained as an apothecary and was often called Dr Dodd. He managed Slade's store and accounts, and made sure there was a good supply of medicines. He was appointed as a Special Constable to be available for duty should the need arise. He may have been responsible for writing up the Magistrate's notes such as the 1849 Census and other annual reports to the Colonial Secretary. At the end of that year Slade wrote with some asperity that Drummond of 'Hawthornden' was tardy in handing in his returns, while Phillips of 'Culham' refused to give any information. Also James Clinch had not made any application for a pastoral lease of land on which he had squatted. Clinch had become an independent owner of sheep and made his application in January at Perth securing a very large area. By 1849 he was shepherding six times more sheep than Slade owned.

Slade was having financial trouble. Apart from falling prices for wool and sandalwood, a disastrous flood along the Avon in 1847 had poured through his cottage making in uninhabitable. They moved into the barn and John Britt was engaged to add two rooms and a verandah to convert it into a new home.

Lt Slade died suddenly in July 1850 and was buried in the south-eastern corner of 'Glen Avon'. His son Frederick was only twelve years old. Mrs Slade managed the property alone until after 1852 when her daughter Elizabeth married Edmund Ralph Brockman. After that he engaged her ticket-of-leave employees and oversaw their labours. A year later her daughter Jane married Rev. George Purvis Pownall and Christina married Alfred Durlacher.

Mrs Slade was a fairly strict Baptist and being Scottish she had a reputation for being 'a bit close with money', which was to be understood since 'Glen Avon' was heavily mortgaged. Nevertheless in 1850 she offered an acre of land for the building of a church, possibly near where her husband was buried. The offer fell through because she did not hold title to the land.

When Rev. Wollaston paid a visit in 1851 he held divine service in her home. At another service two years later, he was preaching to 'about thirty respectable people'. The bond class may have been excluded. Mrs Slade then gave Wollaston a written guarantee for the use of one of her buildings for church services. In 1856 he found it was in a shameful condition and had no hesitation in telling Mrs Slade and her son-in-law Rev. Pownall of his displeasure.

In January 1859 Mrs Slade was thrown out of her sulky and died. Her son Frederick at twenty-one years of age became manager at 'Glen Avon'. A destructive flood in 1862 damaged the homestead. Several of the employees' cottages were washed away. Only Johnson, the blacksmith and Dodd the storeman remained. Frederick Slade went to live with his sister Mrs Brockman at 'Seabrook' near Northam.

The youngest daughter Agnes accompanied the Pownalls when they returned to England in 1863. They visited Henry Slade at his home 'Blewburton House' and gave him all the news of his colonial acquaintances including Cooke, Dempster, Foley, Herbert and Clinch. As a result Henry Slade wrote to James Clinch and commended him upon his progress as a pastoralist.

Frederick Slade leased 'Glen Avon' to James Wilkerson of 'Katrine' who was seeking other employment after Simeon Viveash assumed management there. In time Wilkerson became the owner of 'Glen Avon' and other smaller properties. He restored the old buildings and made extensive additions to the homestead. He was a fine example of an employee who became a very respected and successful landowner.

In 1866 Moondyne Joe and three other escapees from prison terrorised the Toodyay community. While hiding in the rough hills along the Avon Valley down river from Toodyay they robbed people time and again gathering food, guns, ammunition and civilian clothing. They planned to ride to South Australia and their robberies began at 'Glen Avon' where they held old Dodd and his wife at gunpoint, avoiding the Wilkersons at the homestead where they would meet with tougher resistance. The police finally caught the robbers after a lengthy chase at a place now known as Westonia.

James Wilkerson financed several pastoral stations in the Northwest after his son Charles went there in 1865 with Sam Viveash and Edward Middleton. His other sons helped at 'Glen Avon'. After George Wilkerson

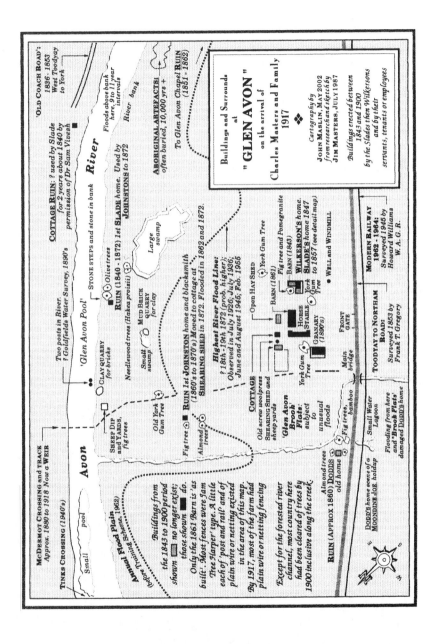

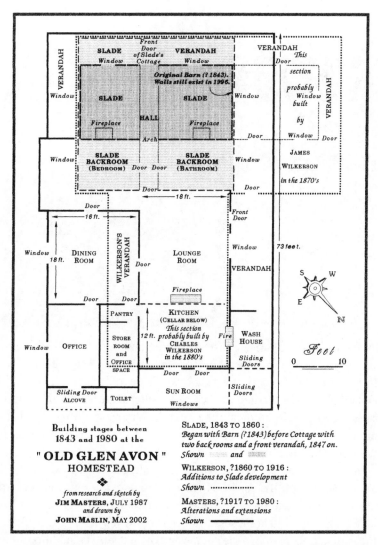

Building stages between
1843 and 1980 at the

" OLD GLEN AVON "
HOMESTEAD

❖

from research and sketch by
JIM MASTERS, JULY 1987
and drawn by
JOHN MASLIN, MAY 2002

SLADE, 1843 TO 1860 :
*Began with Barn (?1843) before Cottage with
two back rooms and a front verandah, 1847 on.*
Shown ▒▒▒▒ *and* ▓▓▓▓

WILKERSON, ?1860 TO 1916 :
Additions to Slade development
Shown ···············

MASTERS, ?1917 TO 1980 :
Alterations and extensions
Shown ————————

married in 1878 he leased 'Oaklands' from his father and later moved
to 'Katrine' where he died. Samuel who married in 1891 also left 'Glen
Avon'. Charles then came back from the Northwest to manage his father's
property and old James Wilkerson retired to Northam. The Wilkersons
were related by marriage to members of the Betts and Sinclair families,
and three Wilkersons married three of the Smiths from 'Baylie Farm'.

Charles Wilkerson benefited from the improved market for farm
produce for the Goldfields and introduced new machinery and farming
methods at 'Glen Avon',. He died suddenly from a fall from his horse
in 1909 predeceasing his father by five years. 'Glen Avon' was sold to

Old barns still in use.
Courtesy Masters family.

J. Wilkerson and his new implements. Distant view of the homestead.

Charles Masters. Charles Masters' son James born in 1917 inherited 'Glen Avon'. Apart from listening avidly to old men like Richard Smith telling stories of the early years, he was a devoted naturalist and bird watcher. He made detailed studies of weather patterns dating from the earliest records. He predicted the cycle of dry years in the 1970s and dammed the Avon River to secure water for his stock. To his delight the large pool attracted birds.

The homestead at 'Glen Avon' was enlarged by Masters and the gardens were carefully tended. There was room for his collection of birds' eggs, his records and precious collection of books. All were lost in 1984 when the historic old homestead was burnt down. The original old walls which still stood, revealed the succession of changes and additions made to 'Glen Avon' homestead. A ground plan was made with the hope that one day it may be rebuilt just as it was.

References
Wollaston's Albany Journals 1848-1856, Collected by Rev. Canon A. Burton, Paterson Brokensha Ltd, Perth, 1954.

Ian Elliot, *Moondyne Joe, the Man and the Myth*, Second ed., Hesperian Press, Carlisle, WA, 1998.

Letter to Clinch from Henry Slade. By kind permission of descendants of John Britt.

Lengthy correspondence with plan etc and interviews between Rica Erickson and J.R. Masters.

12. DUMBARTON

Major Nairn's grant 'Dumbarton' (Avon Location U1 of 1200 acres) lacked an adequate supply of water and was deemed to be too small for free range pasturing. He leased McDermott's grant (Location U of 5000 acres) partly because he believed it included Gabbigin Spring near its eastern boundary. Like many grants in the district the boundaries were not yet surveyed.

'Dumbarton'.
The old windows replaced
by glass doors.
Photograph: Robyn Taylor
2003.

'Dumbarton'. 1920s.
Courtesy Shire of Toodyay.

Apparently he held the lease of Location U with the option of purchase. In June 1839 he advertised in the *Perth Gazette* the sale or lease of 'Mountain Park', commonly called McDermott's grant, stating it was well-equipped as a farm, with a newly-built house with two bedrooms, a sitting room and a storeroom with the necessary outbuildings. Applications were to be forwarded to the proprietor at Maddington Park in the Canning district.

Henry Slade became the lessee. The land was across the river from Frederick Slade's property 'Katrine'. He engaged Miss Hart as his housekeeper, unaware of her doubtful reputation. The recession years of the early 1840s quite disheartened Henry Slade. He had little to lose when he decided to return to England.

The next to lease Nairn's property was James B. Sinclair possibly with the option of purchase. According to his children he bought Avon Location U1 for £246 and may have secured it by mortgaging the property. He named it 'Dumbarton'.

Sinclair and his wife and young son came to the colony in 1840. He was a shepherd indentured to Lionel Lukin and was in debt to him for the clothing required on the voyage. The sum of £246 was the equivalent of more than ten years wages. He may have bought the property with assistance from a merchant who held a mortgage over the grant.

Sinclair built a cottage near a ford crossing the Avon River. There was regular seasonal traffic past his door when shepherds brought their flocks from the outstations, and sandalwooders carted their loads to market. Also rations for the shepherds were taken at least monthly to the outstations. Sinclair conducted a wayside inn by the ford and hired a Parkhurst lad named Richard Kirby to shepherd his sheep. Kirby spent the long idle hours watching sheep by carving his name on a big rock with the date 1849 and the outline of a shepherd's crook and a bottle (which all the shepherds carried, filled with tobacco water to treat scabby sheep). Kirby was still shepherding sheep 30 years later for the Dempsters at Esperance.

In 1849 Mrs Sinclair's brother Charles Glass brought his family to the colony. They stayed at 'Dumbarton' until he found where to settle. Their daughter Janet was born at Sinclair's Bush Inn, late that year and then in 1850 the Glass family moved to Guildford to manage the 'Stirling Arms Hotel'. Before long they too were farming in the Toodyay district.

Flood and fire were ever-present threats. Sinclair's wheat field was in danger in 1848, then in November 1849 the Avon River came very close to the doors of 'Dumbarton'. In November 1850 a bush fire raged through the back country between Toodyay and Northam. Those to agist their flocks elsewhere were Sinclair, Drummond, Wheelock, Whitfield, J.T. Cooke, Clinch and the Gooch brothers, who were leasing 'Mountain Park'.

James B. Sinclair taught his children at home and also conducted a private school for neighbours' children. He was appointed to the Toodyay Education Board in 1875 and served on the Toodyay Roads Board from 1872 to 1895. He built a fine two-storey house by the riverside and enlarged his land holdings, planning to settle each of his nine children on farms of their own when they married.

The eldest son James William, the only one of Scottish birth, sailed to Britain in 1858 to visit relatives. He came back with a wife, Florinda

Stewart. Their home was at 'Blink Bonnie', at the eight-mile post on the Toodyay-Guildford Road. He was only forty-three years old when he died in 1888 at Albany while on his way to Victoria. Other siblings married members of families in the Toodyay district such as J.T. Smith, Wilkerson, Morrell, Lloyd, Ferguson and McCluney. The youngest son William Robert was managing 'Dumbarton' when his father died in 1899 without leaving a will. Having cared for the old man for several years he claimed the property. An older brother disputed this. Florinda at Blink Bonnie also feared the loss of that property. When these matters were brought to the law courts both William Robert and Florinda won their rights.

References

P.W.H. Theil, *Twentieth Century Impressions of Western Australia*, 1901. Reprinted Hesperian Press, Carlisle, 2000.

A.T. Thomas, *History of Toodyay*, The Toodyay Road Board, 1949.

Mary Bentley, *The Morgan Family* 1780-1986. Privately published.

Various newspaper reports on court cases published in November and December 1905.

Lukin papers, courtesy Lionel Lukin and interviews.

'Shepherds Rock'.
Courtesy Shire of Toodyay.

13. OAKLANDS AND NEUGIN

'Oaklands' and 'Neugin' (McDermott's grant Location U of 5000 acres) were named in 1867. The original owner was Captain James McDermott who married Nancy Turner, daughter of the pioneers at Augusta. They lived at Fremantle where he had a store. A daughter Elizabeth Ann was born there in 1833 and Nancy was pregnant with a son when Captain McDermott and his crew were drowned in a storm off Safety Bay.

'Neugin'.
Photograph: Robyn Taylor
2003.

Early cottage at 'Neugin'.
Photograph: Robyn Taylor
2003.

Nancy took Elizabeth Ann and baby son James to live with her parents at Augusta, leasing the grant to Major Nairn. At Augusta she was wooed persistently by an old admirer Dr Alfred Green. She resisted his advances for he was an alcoholic, but in 1844 she agreed to the marriage. Her son disliked his stepfather. She was well-educated and had received tuition also in France, so she was capable of teaching her children, but by the time James approached the age of fifteen years she sent him to Albany to be tutored in preparation for entering a college in England. She wrote long letters to him knowing that while Dr Green was alive he would resist the thought of returning to Western Australia. It was about this time that the grant in the Avon district reverted back from Major Nairn to the Dermott's.

On the few occasions when Nancy and her daughter left Augusta to visit Perth together they were among the gentry at official and social gatherings. At a grand ball they met George Whitfield of Toodyay and after a brief courtship Elizabeth Ann married him in 1856.

Dr Green was recently appointed as the District Medical Officer at Toodyay so they travelled together and for some weeks shared accommodation there while George Whitfield prepared a home for his bride. He owned a small block of land by the Avon near the McDermott's grant and soon had his cottage ready for occupation. At this time he may have been involved in the management of Location U where he cut a large quantity of sandalwood. He had other leases in the vicinity during the late 1840s which also yielded sandalwood.

Dr Green was dismissed from his Toodyay position because of his addiction for alcohol, despite a petition signed by several prominent settlers. He and his wife Nancy then occupied Location U which she named 'Val d'Esperance' or 'Hope Valley'. Several men of the bond class were employed including Lester Dennis, George Allingham, Michael Lawler (who died in 1865) and Henry Branch (who died in 1867).

In the meantime Nancy Green received letters from her son James McDermott. He left England to join those in America who were fighting in the Civil War. Also he was married to a young widow, Hannah Cooley, who had a crippled son named Alvin. Then came news that a son Charles was born to them in 1861 and James in 1862.

Nancy's daughter Elizabeth Ann Whitfield wrote to her brother James McDermott telling of her concern when their mother's health began to fail. James set sail with his family and arrived in the colony in October 1867, only to learn of Nancy's death some weeks before. He then claimed Avon Location U as his inheritance and Dr Green then married Nancy's sister and went to live at Northam.

James McDermott was very critical of the condition of his property and also of George Whitfield who had cut so much valuable sandalwood from it. He commissioned John Morrell of Northam to build a bigger house and named it 'Oaklands' after his place of residence in the United States of America. His two sons walked to 'Katrine School' five miles away. As soon as they were old enough to help on the farm they were set to work. Charles was only a youth when he was sent to Guildford in charge of a load of sandalwood.

Charles married Jane Ferguson in 1886 and built a home on the portion of Location U which he would inherit naming it 'Neugin'. His brother James married his cousin Anna Louise Whitfield and built his home closer to his father's. After his mother died in 1888 James urged his father to come and live with them, but it was only after the old man's house was burnt down that the offer was accepted.

Old James McDermott died in 1910 and was buried in the historic Nardie cemetery where his mother Nancy and so many of the family were laid to rest.

References

Tom Turner, *Turners of Augusta*, Paterson Brokensha Pty Ltd., Perth, 1956.

Barbara King, *Through the Seventh Gate*, Acton Press, Perth, 1994.

Toodyay Resident Magistrate's Records, CSO 368, 29 Sept. 1856 WAA. Battye Library.

14. NEWGAIN.

'Newgain', James Twine's property in the Toodyay district was a combination of several small adjacent grants. He had arrived in the colony at the age of twenty in the *Cygnet* in 1833 with the group of Methodists who settled at 'Tranby' in the Swan district. At first he was employed by Dr Harris, one of the 'Tranby' group, but soon owned a small farm at Middle Swan, next door to Dr Viveash's property. He married and had two sons.

'Newgain'.
Photograph: Robyn Taylor 2003.

James Twine's wife was a widow with two sons of her own who inherited their father's land in the Toodyay district near land owned by Dr Viveash. Twine and Viveash exchanged their land holdings in order to consolidate their properties.

By the 1850s, Twine was living on the Toodyay property that he appropriately named 'Newgain'. In 1854 he joined the newly formed Agricultural Society and was a successful competitor in their first show. He held pastoral leases in the back country between Toodyay and Northam where his sons and stepsons could shepherd his sheep. When a flood in 1857 washed away most of the fords across the Avon he was one of the settlers who offered to cart stone to build a higher ford at 'Nardie'. He employed ticket-of-leave labourers to put up buildings and

Twine family outside 'Newgain' house, ca.Christmas 1903.
Old Gaol Museum,
Shire of Toodyay Collection.

fence his 1400 acre property and could boast he had one of the biggest farms in the Toodyay district.

When James Twine's elder son married in 1863 he became more involved in the management of 'Newgain'. He sent his children to Sinclair's school at Dumbarton. Twine's younger son Alfred George who married in 1867, lived at 'Maisemore', another farm that was part of the original Viveash land. He was not so fortunate with his children, some died in infancy or later by accident.

James Twine did not participate in later Agricultural Shows at Toodyay but his name does appear linked with that of Alfred in the 1869 list of exhibitors.

In 1870 after the British Government decided against sending more convicts to the colony the Government introduced a system of road management by local people. When Road Board elections were held in Toodyay in February 1871, James Twine won a seat which he retained until the end of 1874. Thereafter he was content to retire and leave the management of his properties to his sons.

15. KNOCKDOMINIE

'Knockdominie' (Avon Location U2 of 4029 acres) was granted to Captain Francis Whitfield in 1836. He had four adult sons who may have built a slab hut on the grant. When Whitfield was offered the position of Resident Magistrate in the newly opened district of Toodyay a mud brick cottage was built to accommodate his wife as well. It resembled that at 'Newleyine' with a stone chimney and a loft reached by a ladder for sleeping quarters. The kitchen floor was notable for the flooring of flat slabs of stone.

'Knockdominie'.
Courtesy Shire of Toodyay.

Captain Whitfield did not take up residence and assume official duties until February 1838. The delay was caused by the absence from the colony of the Resident Magistrate of York, with whom he needed to confer on the boundary between the two districts.

Owners of some of the large grants at Toodyay were anxious to sell or lease their land, regarding them more as an investment than a place of residence. To secure the titles to the grants some improvements had to be made and few wished to go so far from settlements along the Swan Valley. Some of these men commissioned Resident Magistrate Whitfield to show prospective buyers of their Toodyay grants.

Whitfield's sons owned sheep and contemplated leasing Dr Waylen's grants (Locations 4 and 11). Instead they went to York and leased the Clarkson grant at York known as 'Wilberforce'. This change of plans may have been caused by an incident at Waylen's grant when Aborigines attacked his shepherds at their hut and an Aborigine was killed.

A settler's first concern was to grow enough wheat to keep his family in flour for a year. He had to be as self-sufficient as possible since cartage from Guildford was very costly. Aborigines' food was from the game they hunted. They burnt the bush to promote fresh growth that would attract game to their territory. They also burnt the bulrushes near the swamps and waterholes. These activities took place at the height of summer to enable the women to harvest the tubers of the bulrush which they named as *yanjettee*.

The risk of losing a crop of wheat in summer was reduced when Whitfield levied the Toodyay settlers for wheat to be given to the Aborigines to induce them to delay their summer burns until after harvest. The Governor also offered grain and blankets. Whitfield then urged the Governor to authorise the building of roads to connect 'Knockdominie' with the outlying settlers at 'Mountain Park' and 'Hawthornden'.

In September 1839 Mrs Whitfield went to Guildford to stay with her daughter, Mrs G.F. Stone, who was expecting a baby in December. This was the Whitfield's first grandchild and Mrs Whitfield stayed to assist her daughter until January 1840. During her absence she left the housekeeping duties at 'Knockdominie' to a young servant girl who became pregnant. When the child was born in July the girl killed the baby and was convicted of concealing a birth. There was some sympathy for the girl. Whitfield and his sons were implicated, and Captain Whitfield who took the blame was ostracised by polite society.

Whitfield resigned his duties as Resident Magistrate and advertised in October 1840 of his intention to auction his furniture and stock before leaving the colony. 'Knockdominie' was already mortgaged to Thomas Mellersh in July and the titles to the grant were transferred to his two eldest sons, Francis (1812-1889) and George Munro (1815-1890).

However Whitfield could not raise the funds to leave the colony so he lived alone in a small cottage at 'Knockdominie'. In January 1842 the grant was leased to William Dodd, an apothecary who advertised in the *Inquirer* offering to take sheep there on shares and guaranteeing to keep them free of the scab disease which was spreading through the flocks in the Swan River districts. The partnership between the Whitfield brothers was terminated in 1843, six months before Francis married Eliza Shaw and went to live at 'Ninego', the eastern portion of 'Knockdominie' to be known later as 'Wicklow Hills'. The mortgage on the grant was transferred to William Tanner and when he left the colony it was placed in

Samuel Moore's hands. Moore's untimely death in 1849 left his financial affairs in disarray. For a time Francis Whitfield faced foreclosure but was saved by the sandalwood trade.

George who suffered from ill health soon sold his share to Francis and secured rights to cut sandalwood by taking out a 4000 pastoral lease along the eastern boundary of 'Knockdominie' as well as the lease of McDermott's property. He also took up a large leasehold along the Lower Moore River in partnership with his younger brother Edward.

Like so many young men in the colony in the early 1850s these three brothers sailed to the Victorian gold diggings leaving their pastoral interests in the hands of Thomas Whitfield. They returned in 1853 quite disillusioned by their experiences. In 1854 Thomas took up a large pastoral lease at Yandanooka, while Francis continued to hold the Moore River lease.

George and Edward continued leasing land along the eastern boundaries of 'Knockdominie'. They worked together until George decided to marry in May 1856. He bought forty acres of land (Locations 174 and 175) near the southern boundary of 'Knockdominie', on the bank of the Avon River opposite 'Nardie'. He took his bride Ann Elizabeth McDermott to live there in a small mud brick cottage and planned to begin farming there.

He was an innovator and thought to make some money by contracting to thresh and winnow neighbours' crops. Previously in 1847 he had bought a newly invented reaping machine from South Australia but it had no brakes and damaged the crop. Also according to a report in the *Inquirer* 12 May 1847 the combs were too close. He sold it to James Drummond Jr who made the necessary improvements to the machine.

Years later when these machines were modified George imported a reaper from England, packed with corks which could be sold at a good price. His wife wrote on 18 November 1862 that the reaping machine was working very well. It could harvest five acres a day and in the same time thresh 150 bushels of grain. When bushfires threatened a farmer's crop George hired his machine to neighbours at a very high charge, leaving his own crop to be reaped with a sickle and scythe.

Francis Whitfield also owned a threshing machine which kept him very busy. His mother-in-law wrote in July 1859 about that 'all-consuming, ever-craving threshing machine' but admitted it was a good way of getting the wheat in, instead of having it 'exposed to all the depradations of time and also wild beasts'.

Francis Whitfield's wife died in 1873. He then sold 'Wicklow Hills' to Dan Connor and joined his son Francis on their Moore River property.

Both George and Francis mortgaged their properties to Dan Connor during the droughts of the late 1860s. In 1871 when the Toodyay Road Board was created George was happy to accept the offer of employment as Superintendent of Works. His wife and family then moved to a substantial building in town. The job lasted only a year or two, after which his wife opened a private school there. Having been taught all the requirements of a refined young lady by her mother she was well qualified as a teacher. She in turn taught her daughter who carried on the school in the Whitfield home until she married her cousin James McDermott Jr in 1887. George Whitfield died in 1890 and his wife in 1924.

References:

Barbara King, *Through the Seventh Gate*, Acton Press,1994. 1984.

Tom Turner, *Turners of Augusta*, Paterson Brokensha Pty Ltd., Perth, 1956.

Samuel Moore's papers. Copies in the hands of the author by kind permission of Joanna Seabrook.

Interviews with Anita Thurman, a granddaughter of George Munro Whitfield and copies of family correspondence in her hands.

16. NARDIE AND CALBALINE

'Nardie' and 'Calbaline' (Avon Location V of 4000 acres) was granted to James Lloyd (1798-1844) a silk dyer by trade. He brought his wife and family to the colony in 1831 and opened a victualling business in Fremantle. He leased his Avon Valley grant known as 'Nardie' to Charles Harper in 1839. Harper was a newcomer to the colony and he was willing to pay £30 per annum as rental. This was slightly more than a labourer's annual wage. Harper buried a baby daughter and one of the Whitfield children in a corner of the property near 'Nardie Pool'.

During the 1840s there was little profit in Lloyd's Fremantle business and it is possible that he was ill. In 1844 he sailed for England taking his wife and eight children and died there in 1844. His widow Hannah returned to Fremantle in 1847 with only three of her children, Hannah (who was seventeen years old and able to help her in a store which she conducted), her son Charles who was ten and Joseph Morris who was born in 1845 after his father's death.

Widow Lloyd extended Harper's lease of 'Nardie' until about 1855. He farmed in a small way and had some sheep. By this time Charles Lloyd, at eighteen years of age, was old enough to manage the Lloyd grant. The property was to be divided between him and his brother Joseph Morris Lloyd. Charles chose the western half named 'Calbaline' while Joseph Morris Lloyd received 'Nardie'. Joseph remained at Fremantle where at the age of twelve he could be apprenticed to a trade. He began working with a builder before going to his share of the property.

Charles Lloyd married Jane Sinclair of 'Dumbarton' in 1862 while Joseph Morris Lloyd married her sister Catherine in 1866. Both were to have large families. Charles' third son David at about nine years of age was already helping to fold the sheep at night. He was destined to spend most of his early life at a shepherd's hut on the family pastoral lease east of Goomalling. He had little schooling. As he said in his old age he 'left school before he started'. He married Sarah Susan Waters in 1897 and was one of the first to buy a farm block in the Coondle Estate when it was subdivided in 1898. This he sold later to a Chinese gardener and then lived in town.

Joseph Morris Lloyd's eldest son Morris, who was three years older than his cousin David, fared much better. He was educated and teamed up with a building contractor, encouraged no doubt by his father who had learned the trade in his youth. Morris and his building partner were employed on buildings as far away as Victoria, Tasmania and New Zealand. Morris married a Victorian and on his return to Toodyay went into partnership with J. H. Wroth to build the Newcastle (Toodyay) Hospital. They also won the contract to build seventy-four cottages for railway employees along the line from Northam to Southern Cross.

By 1900 Morris Lloyd the builder was settled at Toodyay managing 'Nardie' where he built a brick house with seven rooms and spacious verandahs. He planted a vineyard, made wine and was one of the first in the district to own a tractor. His brother Joseph Arthur married Elizabeth Jane Waters adding yet another knot in the growing relationships which tied Toodyay families together. In addition to all their Sinclair relatives they counted among their cousins, Chitty, Wroth and Twine families.

References:
Mercer, F. R., *The Life of Charles Harper of Woodbridge, Guildford, WA*, Westralian Farmers Co-operative Printing Works, 1958.
Interviews with David Lloyd, Henry Ferguson and Judy Hamersley.

17. BRAYBROOK

'Braybrook' was built about 1856-57 near the Convict Depot for Charles Harper (born in 1799). Harper was an English barrister who owned a house in London and in 1837 married Julia Lukin. Her brother Lionel had a grant of land in the Swan River Colony and was to marry Jane Cruikshank a few weeks after his sister's marriage. The two couples sailed from London and arrived at Swan River Colony in December that year.

'Braybrook' deserted in the 1940s and demolished for railway construction.

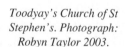

Toodyay's Church of St Stephen's. Photograph: Robyn Taylor 2003.

Lukin's grant of land was at Toodyay, while Harper leased 'Nardie' from the Lloyd family. At this time a wool trade was just developing between New South Wales and London. The two couples hoped to make a living as pastoralists but these hopes faded during the trade recession of the 1840s. Then to add to Harper's troubles the cottage at 'Nardie' used by their Chinese cook was burnt down in 1847.

Harper was a scholarly man with strong religious views. When his infant daughter died in 1839 he buried her near their cottage and read the burial service at the graveside. He performed the same duties when the Whitfield's young daughter was buried there. In 1848 Bishop Short of Adelaide visited Toodyay. Harper needed little persuasion to go to Adelaide to study for the ministry. He was ordained in 1849 and returned to 'Nardie' to serve a parish that extended as far south as York, where a church had been built in 1843. By 1851 a church was built at Northam and plans were in hand to build another on land given by S. P. Phillips of 'Culham' up the Toodyay Valley.

Having vacated 'Nardie', Harper's family went to Perth to live with their relatives the Lukins, while Harper was given temporary residence in one of the new Pensioner Guard cottages at Toodyay.

In 1853 Harper had secured ten acres of land (Avon Location 111) beside the Hiring Depot's new site. The land was in his name and had been bought for Church purposes. He subsequently received permission from the authorities in Perth to buy this land for his own private use. His home 'Braybrook' was built with bricks made by the expiree George Henry Hasell.

In 1857 the Harper family was reunited in their new commodious house, large enough to accommodate guests. Among them was Mrs Phillips who noted in her diary that year that their family stayed overnight at 'Braybrook' on their way to Perth.

After the new town of Newcastle was established around the depot in 1860, Harper's parishioners readily co-operated in the building of St Stephen's Church near the bridge. The builders were George Hasell and another expiree, the stonemason Esau Wetherall.

Harper taught his children at home. By 1861 they had reached adulthood. Having no land for his son Charles to inherit he planned a career for him in the Civil Service. However he was disappointed when the lad was not diligent in his studies. Charles Harper Jr preferred the open-air life as a farmer or pastoralist. He realised this ambition in 1857 soon after meeting Augustus Lee Steere at a housewarming party held at 'Culham' by Squire Phillips and his wife. Charles Jr. was only sixteen years old in 1858 but he went into partnership with Lee Steere and set out to manage a Beverley property 'Haisethorpe'. He was helped by his mother who used a legacy to give him a horse and cart, a barrel of pork, a gun and £50. This was equivalent in modern values of a second-hand truck and enough money to lease a property for a year. In 1864 he explored far to the east of the Avon, but decided to take up land in the Northwest instead. By 1866 he was in partnership with Samuel Viveash near Roebourne. In 1868 when they found pearl shell on the beach they built a 7 ton boat and entered the pearl fishing business.

After Rev. Harper died in 1872 his daughters conducted a private school at 'Braybrook'. Mrs Harper was a gardening enthusiast and a very successful competitor in the local Agricultural Show. Among the native plants grown in her garden was *Eucalyptus macrocarpa*, known as 'Rose of the West'. Marianne North, a celebrated painter of strange and beautiful wildflowers, visited Mrs Harper especially to see this plant.

Mrs Harper wrote long letters to her son Charles while he was in the Northwest informing him of all the family news. There was plenty to tell since she was a Lukin before her marriage and the Lukins at 'Deepdale' were marrying into families such as Phillips, Viveash, Bostock, Dr Ferguson and Clarkson.

Charles Harper became a prosperous man. In 1878 he was elected to the Legislative Council as a representative for the Northwest. He sold his interest in the Northwest that year and moved to Guildford, having married Fanny de Burgh. He bought an interest in the *West Australian* newspaper and used it to promote improvements in agriculture. In 1885 he built a fine home named 'Woodbridge', which many years later became a prestigious National Trust property. Julia Harper died in 1889, and old Mrs Harper died in 1898. Sarah and Mary Harper remained at 'Braybrook' until Mary's death in 1917 after which Sarah reluctantly agreed to leave the old home and move nearer to her brother Charles at Guildford.

'Braybrook' was demolished about 1963 when the wide gauge railway was constructed through the Avon Valley. St Stephens Church stands as a more lasting memorial to Rev. Charles Harper and his family.

References:

Mercer, F. R., *The Life of Charles Harper of Woodbridge, Guildford, WA*, Westralian Farmers Co-operative Printing Works, 1958.

Wollaston's Albany Journals 1848-1856, Collected by Rev. Canon A. Burton, Paterson Brokensha Ltd, Perth, 1954.

Sophie Phillips Diary. Mitchell Library NSW and Battye Library WA.

Interviews with descendants, Judy Hamersley and Mrs C.W. Harper who gave permission to use the family letters.

The Dictionary of Western Australians, WABI File on employers of ticket-of-leave men.

Correspondence with Rev. Paul Atkins 1971.

18. DANIEL CONNOR AND HIS MILL.

Connors Mill.
Photograph: Beth Field, 2003.

Daniel Connor (1832-1898) arrived in the colony as a convict in 1853. By 1870, through his shrewd business dealings, he became one of the most influential men in the Toodyay district. He bought a small block of land at Guildford where in 1859 he took his bride Catherine Conway, a goodhearted illiterate Irishwoman.

The land at Guildford was a holding paddock for the stock he bargained for. A lot of his trade was conducted as a hawker, along the Avon and Toodyay Valleys. He carried needles and thread, ribbons and other small articles in a red handkerchief hanging from a stick over his shoulder. The settlers soon suspected him of sharp dealings and the purchaser of unbranded poddy calves.

In the late 1850s Connor attempted to establish his business at Toodyay but the residents opposed these moves and declined to sell their town blocks to him, believing that in his business dealings he was 'capable of uttering the most gross falsehoods'.

In 1861 when town blocks were offered for sale at the Newcastle townsite he thanked the Toodyay residents for their opposition and bought several blocks at the new townsite where he opened a store. By 1870 he was building a Steam Mill competing against James Drummond whose mill had served the community since 1857.

Connor employed George Hasell as his builder. Other expirees on his payroll were four ticket-of-leave men, Michael Macnamara as brickmaker, and three carpenters named Henry Brocklesby, John Richardson and Herbert Davis. Some of these were recognised at length as worthy citizens and given the right to become members of societies which previously excluded them.

When the Convict Establishment transferred all road and bridge building to the Colonial government the Legislative Council passed the Municipality Act in 1871. Eighteen districts were listed as eligible, but only seven, including Toodyay and Victoria Plains, accepted the responsibility of electing road committees which were then known as Roads Boards.

All men, bond or free, who owned or leased property above a certain value were eligible to vote for members on the Roads Boards. Dan Connor was elected to the Toodyay Roads Board in 1871, and when the Toodyay Municipal Council was established in 1877 he became a member, retaining his seat in both bodies until his death in 1898.

After James Drummond's death in 1873 Daniel Connor borrowed a large sum of money and bought 'Hawthornden' and 'Mt Anderson'. He held mortgages over Whitfield's grant and had an interest in the Coondle and Norman Estates. In 1874 he bought the 'Freemasons Hotel', later to be sold to Thomas Donegan.

As a member of the Toodyay Education Board he shared with Squire Phillips and his wife the duties of examining the pupils of the schools in the district. Connor was the most popular among the pupils who were in awe of Phillips but looked forward to the lollipops that Connor took to sweeten the ordeal of the inspection. He knew the value of education and hired a scholarly ticket-of-leave man named James Hubbard to teach his own children.

Connor had an interest in the North Newcastle suburb being promoted by B. D. Clarkson and built brick houses for rental on the Lots which he owned. By then he was given the nickname of 'The King of Newcastle'. He saw greater opportunities for financial advancement in Perth when the gold rush was at its height in the 1890s. He bought land and property there and built a fine town house. He became a director on the boards of several large financial institutions and was accepted socially in good company where his convict origins were ignored or unknown.

Connor's wife preferred the simpler life at her comfortable brick house beside the Flour Mill. She was well loved for her kindness towards those in trouble and was remembered for the occasions she thwarted Connor's harsher dealings during periods of drought and hardship.

Connor's children's futures were well provided for. His sons studied for medicine at Dublin University. A daughter, Theresa, with her husband Timothy F. Quinlan were installed as managers of the popular Shamrock Hotel in Perth. Another daughter Monica and her husband Edward Hayes managed his 'Wicklow Hills' property at Toodyay.

Daniel Connor died in 1898 having achieved more than anyone thought possible when he arrived as a convict in 1853. His wife in her old age was placed in the care of nuns at the Toodyay Convent which was built largely by benefactions from her children. Connor's rise in society can be traced from official documents which over the years he signed as a stockdealer, storekeeper, miller and finally as a gentleman. His family erected a handsome monument over his grave in the East Perth cemetery. In Toodyay his monument is the historic flour mill he built in 1870.

Connor's Flour Mill has a history of its own. The first miller to be employed there was Charles Marris. He had worked previously at James Drummond's Flour Mill until the 1870 flood washed away his cottage.

In 1891 Marris built his own Union Flour Mill of galvanised iron. This was burnt down a few years later and he then rented Connor's Mill until 1917 after which he and his sons moved to operate a more modern mill at Katanning.

Connor's Mill was then bought by C. M. Lukin who invested a lot of capital fitting it up as a powerhouse to provide electricity for the town. Hitherto people and the street lamplighter used kerosine lamps. A fire in the building in 1927 ruined Lukin and the Mill was left derelict until the Toodyay Tourist Bureau was located there. After that it became a museum displaying machinery.

References

Minutes of the Toodyay Road Board, Battye Library.

Minutes of the Toodyay Municipal Council, Battye Library.

Toodyay Herald, 22 Dec. 1888 10 May 1891.

Resident Magistrate's letters C50 487. Feb. 1861, Public Record Office, State Library.

Communication from a descendant of Charles Marris.

Records of *Western Australian Biographical Dictionary* in the Battye Library regarding Employers of Ticket-of-Leave men.

19. CEMETERIES AT TOODYAY

Cemeteries are important sources of information when researching family trees, but it is wise to check the dates quoted on headstones with those of church records and the Registrar General. For instance Frederick Slade of 'Glen Avon' was buried on his grant in 1850, and was re-interned at the Katrine Cemetery many years later with the date of death 1849 inscribed in the headstone.

Provision had been made for a cemetery at the first Toodyay townsite in 1849 at a place along Wellington Street now known as Cemetery Hill. The choice of this land for burials was unfortunate because the ground was so stony that graves could be only two or three feet deep. Possibly the only person known to be buried there was Michael Barry in 1856. This was unconsecrated ground. In 1857 the Catholic priest was successful in having land for a cemetery (Lot 67) beside the site of the Toodyay church he was about to build. This was deserted after Newcastle was gazetted and the next Catholic cemetery was allotted there. This also was used for only a few years. A number of burials were made on private properties and like those early Toodyay graves are scarcely discernible except for the low mounds of earth.

The cemetery where Charles Harper buried an infant daughter at 'Nardie' in 1839 has been mentioned already. When Francis Whitfield's four-year-old daughter died in 1849 she was buried also at 'Nardie' and the burial service read by Charles Harper at her parents' request. After Harper left 'Nardie' Thomas Millard bought a few acres for a small farm, and was concerned about the possibility of stock trampling on the graves. He offered land around the graves for an official cemetery. Two acres (Location 202) were gazetted in 1857. It became the last resting place for several of the early settlers.

The first burial at St Philips Church at 'Culham' took place in 1860 when the two-year-old son of Squire Phillips was buried. The first burial at St Saviour at 'Katrine' is thought to be that of Robert Rowlands, a carpenter who may have been employed on the building of the church in 1862.

The need for a public cemetery with sections for all creeds was met in 1866 when James Drummond Jr gave land for the purpose. His offer was gladly accepted although there was a mortgage over that area. The first to be buried there was George Slater in 1867. The Catholic

Nardie Cemetery.
Photograph: Robyn Taylor
2002.

Graves at Nardie Cemetery.
Photograph: Robyn Tyalor
2002.

Nancy Green's headstone,
Nardie Cemetery.
Photograph: Robyn Taylor
2002.

Toodyay (Newcastle)
Cemetery.
Photograph: Robyn Taylor
2003.

Plaque commemorating Aboriginal gravesite. Photograph: Robyn Taylor 2003.

Seventh Day Adventist burial ground. Photograph: Robyn Taylor 2004.

Markey headstones in Seventh Day Adventist Cemetery. Photograph: Robyn Taylor 2004.

Cemetery at St Philip's Church, Culham. Photograph: Beth Field.

cemeteries, including the one surveyed in the new town of Newcastle, were no longer used. The graves had been marked by wooden crosses which were eventually destroyed by white ants.

Many of the Drummond family were buried in a private cemetery near their homestead during the period 1840s to 1870s. (Further notes are included in the chapter on 'Hawthornden'.)

About the turn of the century two more cemeteries came into prominence. A small Seventh Day Adventist Cemetery is located down river from 'Deepdale' where several members of the Markey family are buried. The oldest headstone is dated 1930. An Aboriginal burial ground was discovered in 1891 when work began on a proposed railway up the Toodyay Valley. This is located near the bank of the Avon River, downstream from the bridge. Its ethnic origin was determined by the fact that the bodies were buried in upright positions and this was verified by a part-Aborigine William Shaw from York. It is possible these people died of measles during two epidemics in 1861 and 1883-4. The site was reserved in 1889 but was not gazetted until December 1916. A commemorative plaque marks the location of the burial ground.

References
Communications from James Masters.
National Trust records.
Interviews with descendants of James Drummond, Judy Hamersley and Mrs Harper.

20. DONEGAN'S COTTAGE

'Donegan's Cottage' on Lot 101 in the suburb of Toodyay known as North Newcastle was occupied around 1900 by James Donegan (1841-1915). He was the son of Sergeant John Donegan, an Enrolled Pensioner who qualified for a grant of four acres of land (S3) at the Newcastle townsite of Newcastle (renamed Toodyay in 1910). Sergeant Donegan was stationed at Baylup, midway between Toodyay and Guildford, in charge of the road party there.

Donegan's Cottage'.
Photograph: Robyn Taylor 2003.

Young James Donegan was only thirteen years old when he was employed by Squire Phillips at 'Culham', but by 1859 he was leasing a small farm block from James Drummond at 'Hawthornden'. In 1863 he won a contract for carrying the weekly mails between Toodyay and Guildford in 1863. Two years later he married Ellen Cockman. His wife and his mother between them conducted a wayside inn at Baylup. Since travellers usually stopped overnight they were kept very busy, earning a great reputation for their high standard of hospitality.

James Donegan spent much of his time as a mailman between Toodyay and Guildford so he also became responsible for the maintenance of the road. However traffic along the road to Guildford was greatly reduced when the railway from Perth was extended by a spur line from Clackline to Toodyay in 1887. The wayside inn lost most of its custom and James was no longer a mail contractor. He turned instead to carting goods to the newly-discovered Yilgarn goldfield. His family moved from Baylup to the 'Nine Mile Farm' much closer to the town of Toodyay.

James Donegan's brother Thomas owned the 'Freemasons Hotel' by then but was in ill-health so James managed that business for a short time before Thomas died in 1891. Another brother who was a wagoner and road contractor in the same year decided to settle down on a block of land near the bridge over the Avon. This was located on the old road to the former townsite at Toodyay, where suburban blocks had been surveyed. James Donegan bought Lot 101 there. It is possible that a two-roomed mud bat cottage was already there. Some of Drummond's employees had homes along that road in the old days.

It is not known when James Donegan made the additions to the original building. He had five sons but while the eldest, William James, was married in 1890, several were still unwed by 1900. James Donegan's wife died in 1949 and he died in 1954. The cottage was inherited by their son Harold. In 1981 the Toodyay Shire Council bought the house and land for extensions to the Recreation Ground, but Harold was granted tenancy until his death in 1993.

The unoccupied cottage was vandalised, and about to be demolished when the Toodyay Historical Society obtained custody. After much voluntary labour and with the help of a grant and aid from the Shire Council, the cottage was restored and recognised for its heritage value by being entered on the state's Register of Heritage Places. In 2003, 'Donegan's Cottage' became the headquarters of the Toodyay Historical Society. It is representative of a labourer's cottage of the 1800s, few of which remain intact. It is also a memorial to a family that figured largely in the Toodyay district. The Donegans were good cricketers and could field a family team. They defeated the Toodyay team in 1924 and received so much publicity in the newspapers they were challenged by the Watts family team at Guildford, but the Donegans don't treasure any memory of the result of that match.

References
Interviews with several members of the Donegan family.

21. DEEPDALE

'Deepdale' (Avon Location 3 of 4784 acres) was selected originally in 1836 by Governor Stirling and was transferred to Lionel Lukin a year later, under unusual circumstances. Lionel Lukin arrived at Swan River Colony in 1830 and qualified for a grant of land. He chose it in the Murray River area. This was not surveyed for some years so he lived at Fremantle where he opened an inn, invested in a small trading vessel and bought shares in the Fremantle Whaling Company. All these ventures failed. Then when his grant was surveyed it was found to be partly in the sea. He sought to have it located elsewhere but got no satisfaction. He had good reason to believe he was the most unfortunate man in the colony.

'Deepdale'.
Photograph: Robyn Taylor
2002.

'Deepdale'. Photograph
c.1890s.
Courtesy Shire of Toodyay.

In January 1837 he sailed to London to press his claims at a higher level. He had wealthy and influential connections and was gratified to have Stirling's grant allotted to him. It included rich alluvial flats along the Avon with a deep pool of permanent water adjacent to the proposed townsite of Toodyay. He then married Jane Cruikshank and returned to Swan River Colony accompanied by his sister Julia Lukin and her newly-wed husband Charles Harper.

Pastoralists in New South Wales were developing a good trade in wool with the English. Lukin bought some stud sheep of the prized Dorrien breed and sent them to the Avon district to be shepherded by John Gooch. Unfortunately all the lambs were born dead. Undaunted Lukin bought more sheep and sponsored the migration of a Scottish shepherd, James B. Sinclair, who arrived in the colony with his wife and young son early in 1840.

Lukin's list of misfortunes grew. The floods of 1847 and 1849 spread over his rich river flats and in 1849 a disastrous fire made him contemplate selling 'Deepdale' to settle his debts. Another fire raced through all the back country from Toodyay to Northam, which forced many pastoralists to seek good grazing land elsewhere. Lukin secured 8000 acres leasehold along his boundary with the townsite. His decision to stay followed the introduction of convicts in 1850. He anticipated securing provisioning contracts. Then when a Convict Hiring Depot was established at Toodyay another source of income presented itself. The population at Toodyay was increasing rapidly. Lukin had 500 acres of his rich alluvial flats near the townsite surveyed into 10-acre lots to be leased as farmlets. He also leased 'Deepdale' and his 8000 acre pastoral lease to the Gooch family, one of those who lost all their pastures in the bush fires.

Lukin succeeded Michael Clarkson as Superintendent at the Hiring Depot during 1852-3. It may have been during this period that he built a new house on 'Deepdale', situated on high ground and more centrally located in the property. It is highly probable that he used convict labourers with building skills.

In 1854 he was transferred to the Mt Eliza Depot at Perth where his family enjoyed the niceties of living in the capital city. They returned to 'Deepdale' in 1858, the year that old John Gooch died. A small legacy from England enabled Lukin to retire from agricultural pursuits and sell his flocks. His health must have been failing, for he died at 'Deepdale' in 1863 at the age of sixty-two years. Because the Avon was in high flood, Lukin's body could not be conveyed to the Toodyay Cemetery so he was buried near their home where a marble headstone was erected. His widow was pregnant with their thirteenth child.

The eldest son Lionel Boyd Lukin at twenty-two years of age was capable of managing 'Deepdale'. His younger brothers Wilfred and Henry were employed at 'Haisethorpe' (known also as 'Youndegin') east of York, in the charge of their cousin Charles Harper who was leasing the property. A younger brother George Lukin would join Harper who was preparing to leave on a new pastoral venture in the Northwest. Three of the Lukin daughters were married at the time their father died, but his son Lionel Boyd Lukin still had other siblings to care for as well as his mother.

Like most landholders he employed ticket-of-leave men. These were accommodated in huts alongside the farm buildings. In 1870 one of these men, James Douglas, a man of little experience, attempted to smoke out an invasion of fleas from his hut and accidentally set fire to it. Thomas Lee who lived across the river rushed to help. They saved only some articles when the adjacent farm buildings caught fire, destroying machinery, bales of wool and a stack of hay. Douglas was distraught and committed suicide. Lionel B. Lukin could ill-afford such a disaster.

His brothers were faring better. In 1874 young George leased land known as 'Wilgoyne', far to the east of the settled regions. Twenty years later it became a well-patronised stop-over for prospectors flocking to the Yilgarn goldfield. Wilfred Lukin who accompanied his cousin Charles Harper to the Northwest remained there and overlanded sheep to the West Kimberley district. In 1886 he joined the goldrush to Halls Creek but having little luck he sailed to the Yukon goldfield in North America. He was returning home to 'Deepdale' in 1906 but was killed in the earthquake that devastated San Francisco.

Lionel B. Lukin also hoped to better his financial position after the discovery of gold in Western Australia. His river flats were very valuable. They were sold as farmlets. There were enough buyers to warrant the building of a community hall to serve also as a school. After his death in 1912 his son Charles M. Lukin inherited 'Deepdale'. He bought 'Connors Mill' and converted it into an electric power station. It functioned profitably until a fire forced its closure in 1927. He was the third generation of the Lukin family to face ruin because of fire.

References

Lukin family papers per favour of D. Lukin.
Interviews with D. Lukin and D. Munckton.
Inquirer May 1850.
Toodyay Herald 3 July 1907, 12 December 1907, 9 February 1918.
Resident Magistrate's letters re inquest into death of Douglas, State Record Office, CSO 1870.

22. GRANNY CLARKSON'S COTTAGE AND MT ANDERSON.

Jain (Jane) Clarkson (1813-1905) was the eldest daughter of James Drummond the botanist, and was one of those pioneers who came in the *Parmelia* to found the colony in 1829. In 1877 she moved to a cottage near the bridge over the Avon River at Toodyay, in those days known as Newcastle. She remarked to her friend Mrs Harper of 'Braybrook' that this was her nineteenth move and she hoped it would be her last. She was to remain there until her death in 1905. For generations to come her home became known as 'Granny Clarkson's Cottage'.

'Granny Clarkson's Cottage'.
Photograph: Robyn Taylor 2003.

'Granny Clarkson's Cottage' in
a derelict state.
Photograph 1991.
Courtesy John Ainsworth.

An attempt is made here to identify those nineteen moves. Several would have been made before her marriage to Michael Clarkson. She was sixteen years of age when her parents landed at Garden Island in June 1829. The Drummonds then moved to Perth where her father planted cuttings and seedlings. Within a few months he was establishing a Government Garden at Guildford but Governor Stirling soon closed this. The family then lived on their grant at Maylands opposite the Clarksons at 'Tranby'.

The Drummond's home was burnt down in October 1833. By early November Jain Drummond was married to Michael Clarkson. Jain moved to 'Tranby' but two years later she was living at 'Wilberforce' in the York district. Michael's father was with them when he died in 1836. A year or two later 'Wilberforce' was sold to Edward Hamersley and Michael and Jain returned to 'Tranby' where he hoped to make a living as a land agent.

A world recession in trade in the early 1840s nearly ruined many colonists including Michael Clarkson. In 1842 he was grateful to accept an offer of accommodation from Jain's brother James Drummond on his property in the Toodyay Valley. In February 1846 he wrote a letter to a relative in England saying that he was about to begin farming in a small way at 'Nunyle', a small grant near the Drummonds.

As Jain packed their belongings once again she may have wished to settle there at last. They buried a four-year-old son at 'Nunyle' in 1845 and their sixth child Sarah was born there and another son was added to the family in 1849. Michael by then was giving up unprofitable farming at 'Nunyle' and bought a town block at Toodyay where he earned a pittance as postmaster, his duties in this office often performed by Jain.

Michael Clarkson owned a small flock of 500 sheep which he shepherded near the townsite on a lease formerly held by James Drummond. When he was unable to pay for the lease in 1849 he wrote to the authorities in Perth requesting an extension of time until he sold his wool and wethers. His financial troubles were relieved in 1851 when he was appointed as the Superintendent of the Convict Hiring Depot at Toodyay. In 1852 he was transferred to Perth as Assistant Superintendent at the Mt Eliza Hiring Depot, a post he held until 1854.

Michael and Jain then took their family back to Toodyay to begin farming once more at 'Mt Anderson' which was in the hands of James Drummond Jr. He followed Drummond's example of offering small areas of land free of rental to men who were prepared to clear and farm them. Michael employed eight ticket-of-leave men who within a year cleared and ploughed sixty-five acres.

Sons of early colonists who wished to be independent were exploring more distant areas for leasehold. In 1864 Clarkson's son Bernard at the age of twenty-five years joined with young Charles Harper and the Dempster brothers to look at country far to the east of the Avon Valley. Another son Edward Clarkson at the age of seventeen years then took the family flock to an outstation there, some eighty miles away. His brother James took rations regularly to Edward but a year later Edward was speared at his outcamp by Aborigines. His body was brought back to 'Hawthornden' to be buried beside Johnston Drummond who had suffered the same fate at his camp in the Moore River district in 1845.

In 1864 Deborah, the eldest of Michael and Jain's children married a widower Alfred Durlacher who was the Resident Magistrate at Toodyay. They were soon transferred to Geraldton where Deborah's uncles James and John Nicol Drummond had extensive leaseholds at 'Oakabella' and 'White Peak'.

Michael and Jain's son, Barnard Clarkson was still searching for land. In 1866 he sailed to the Kimberley district with some friends, but decided this area was too distant for settlement. Instead he accepted James Drummond's offer of the management of his property 'Oakabella' in the Geraldton area. He married Isabella Lukin in 1867 and after the wedding celebrations at 'Hawthornden' set out with his bride.

Michael Clarkson's prospects were not so bright. After a series of drought years in the 1860s he was heavily in debt. At a meeting of the local Agricultural Society in 1865 he resigned from the Secretaryship saying he was contemplating leaving the district. However his son James carried on as manager at 'Mt Anderson' and Jain was spared the trials of moving once more.

Both Barnard Clarkson and his sister Deborah Durlacher had tragic experiences at Geraldton in 1869. His first-born died at the age of two years while Alfred Durlacher committed suicide rather than face charges of defalcation of Government money paid to him for pastoral leases. Barnard and his family returned to Toodyay to work for his uncle James Drummond and occupied one of the cottages at 'Mill Farm'. Deborah took her children to 'Mt Anderson' to live with her parents.

Jain Clarkson needed Deborah's aid because Michael's health was failing. He died in 1871. Three months later the youngest daughter Sarah married a neighbour Frederick Mackie Roe of 'Roesland'. The cottage at 'Mt Anderson' was then less crowded. Sarah's home at 'Roesland' had been built many years before by a tenant, John Cook Jr. It was renovated prior to the wedding by two ticket-of-leave men, John Richardson, a carpenter and a qualified wood turner named John Murray.

In 1872 James Clarkson married Selina Green. Jain and her daughter Deborah then left 'Mt Anderson' to the newlyweds and moved to one of Drummond's cottages near where Barnard was living, and where his wife gave birth to a second son.

After James Drummond's death in 1873, 'Hawthornden' and 'Mt Anderson' were bought by Daniel Connor who borrowed heavily from a bank where his credit rating was high. 'Vine Cottage' with its cluster of cottages on 'Mill Farm' were bought by the Dempster brothers so these were no longer available to the Clarksons.

At the time of these transactions James Clarkson's wife and infant daughter died. He had no heart to carry on at 'Mt Anderson'. Barnard undertook to continue the lease of the property and when he took his family to the old home he was joined by his mother and sister Deborah with her children.

As Jain grew older she was less tolerant of noisy grandchildren in the crowded rooms at 'Mt Anderson'. In 1877 she moved into a neat cottage near the bridge over the Avon and within walking distance of the town. It was relatively new having been built in 1871 by Drummond's employee Henry Whitaker, an expiree who had left for Geraldton after Drummond's death.

This was Jain's nineteenth move, and as stated above, she had confided to her friend Mrs Harper that she hoped it would be her last. These two aging women shared many confidences because Barnard's wife Isabella Lukin was Mrs Harper's niece. When Mrs Harper wrote to her son Charles, a pioneer of the Northwest, she sent him many items of news of all his numerous cousins, for the Lukins also were a large family, married into several of the leading families in the district.

Jain Clarkson in her last haven was to suffer many sorrows. In 1877 her youngest son William died of a silly prank at a Hamersley party, when he was pushed into a sheep dip. Two months later Barnard's two-year-old daughter was buried in the cemetery within sight of Jain's cottage. Then in May that year Sarah's husband Frederick Mackie Roe died. Sarah was distraught. She took her two troublesome little sons and her ailing baby daughter to 'Mt Anderson' and then to her mother's cottage, waiting to hear whether 'Roesland' would be leased or sold. All were relieved when her brother-in-law James Roe provided her with a home in Perth. Her baby girl died there shortly after.

Barnard was also anxious about his future, fearing that 'Mt Anderson' might be leased to someone else, or sold. When he secured the lease of the property for the next fourteen years, Jain acquainted Mrs Harper with the good news and that he planned to build extensions to their home.

In 1879 Barnard won a seat on the Toodyay Road Board and was commissioned as a J.P. alongside Squire Phillips. The Roads Board meetings were held at the 'Freemasons Hotel' and some members gathered there for a social evening. Barnard hired a private room where gambling sessions were held. Small fortunes were said to be won or lost there. In

*Granny Clarkson at her
cottage with her son James
and daughter Deborah.
Photograph early 1900s.*

*'Mt Anderson Cottage',
rear view, 1900,
Courtesy Shire of Toodyay.*

1880 the Resident Magistrate charged the proprietor, Thomas Donegan for allowing unlawful games to be played on the premises. During the Court hearing Phillips angrily disputed the Resident Magistrate's charge, but Barnard decided he was ineligible to sit in judgement and withdrew. He took no further part in Road Board affairs until he won a seat in 1885, a position he held until 1893.

In 1885 Barnard D. Clarkson mortgaged 'Mt Anderson' for £2700. He planned to subdivide 40 acres of 'Mt Anderson' land near where Jain lived and next to the cemetery. A few tenants already occupied small blocks of about ten acres each along the river but the rest would be surveyed to create about 100 town lots to be named North Newcastle Suburb. This move was prompted by the anticipated growth of the town when a railway was built to Northam. An extension to Newcastle by a spur line was expected to follow. These town lots could be bought at £20 each after survey fees were paid and could return a handsome profit.

Many of those who bought town lots were local people, sons of colonists who made their living as labourers, wagoners and tradesmen. Cricket was their favourite pastime. In 1886 the old ground at the townsite was deemed unsuitable for sport meetings. Barnard Clarkson lent some of his land at North Newcastle for a cricket ground and football matches. These sporting clubs raised the money to keep this land as a Recreation Oval. This may have stimulated the sales of North Newcastle surburban lots. Connor is said to have bought several of these blocks of land and had two-roomed cottages built on them.

The discovery of gold brought crowds of prospectors and many wagoners to travel through the town and to the Yilgarn by way of the sandalwooders' track. More tradesmen including blacksmiths and carriage builders opened up businesses at North Newcastle.

When his mortgage was due to be discharged Barnard D. Clarkson borrowed a larger amount to carry on. Once more the 'Mt Anderson' title deeds were in other hands. Barnard thought he was reasonably secure despite his continued dependence on mortgages.

James Clarkson had not fared so well. Like his father he was not a 'stayer'. He led a lonely life while earning a living as a wagoner and a sandalwooder. When the value of sandalwood dropped he was in debt to the Dempster brothers for goods bought at their store at 'Vine Cottage'. When they offered him work as manager at their Esperance station he sold his horse and dray to them in 1884. He was a quiet likeable man, very industrious and good with sheep and other stock, but they had their reservations about his ability as a manager. He arranged for his wages to be paid to his mother but stayed in the job for only two years.

James and Deborah went to live with their mother Jain to care for her in her old age. When her faculties were failing she dwelt a lot upon the past and if young men visited them she greeted them lovingly, thinking they were her sons who had died long before. She died in 1905 at 92 years of age, a well-respected early colonist. Regretfully no one recorded in detail the 19 moves she made in her lifetime.

Barnard Drummond Clarkson ended his life as a highly esteemed citizen. He cleared his properties of debt and received the titles to 'Mt Anderson' in November 1907. He had been elected as MLA for the Toodyay district in December 1890 serving until his death in March 1909. His sons shared his properties named 'Yandee', 'The Range' and 'Mt Anderson' which was renamed 'Foggarthorpe'.

References
Michael Clarkson's letter 19 February 1846 to W.H. Bellin in England. Copy held by Rica Erickson by favour of a descendant.
State Archives PRO CSO 59/48 February 1848.
Battye Library, Dempster paper MN 558, 19 August 1885 and 12 November 1886.
Newspapers 14 August 1886 and 27 August 1887.
Mrs Harper's letters to Charles 27 February 1877, 13 June 1877, 12 July 1887, courtesy Judy Hamersley.
Interviews with Mrs Olive Atwell, Toodyay.
Certificates at DOLA concerning mortgages on Avon Loc U3 dated 4 July 1885, 12 June 1891 and 15 March 1889.

23. HAWTHORNDEN

'Hawthornden' (Avon Location U4 of 2900 acres) and 'Mill Farm' (Avon Location I2) were granted to James Drummond the botanist (1784-1863) and his son James (1814-1873). The family arrived at Swan River Colony in the *Parmelia* in 1829. James Drummond the elder worked at first as the Government botanist and gardener but within a few years he spent most of his time exploring and collecting specimens of plants for despatch to clients in Europe, while his sons managed the Drummond farms at Maylands and Helena Valley.

'Hawthornden'.
Photograph: Robyn Taylor
2004.

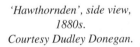

'Hawthornden', side view,
1880s.
Courtesy Dudley Donegan.

After the opening of the Toodyay area for selection his final choice was in the Toodyay Valley.

The Anderson family owned the neighbouring grant U3 but they were planning to sail to Tasmania and offered 900 acres of this land to James Drummond Jr in return for making the improvements which would give them freehold title to the land. This 900 acres was then excised in the name of James Drummond Jr. He also had the use of the whole of Anderson's grant. In 1837 he took the family's flocks and herds to Toodyay and by 1838 the rest of the Drummond family were living on their grant which they named 'Hawthornden'. As already related they were joined by the eldest Drummond daughter Jain and her husband Michael Clarkson in 1844, who began farming at 'Nunyle'.

James Drummond Jr was energetic. He built a barn on his 900 acres and a horse-drawn mill close by, and named his property 'Mill Farm'.

After these improvements the Andersons received the titles to the 'Mt Anderson' land in 1847. James Drummond Jr was still in occupation and it is assumed that he then leased their land with option of purchase.

The Drummond flocks and herds flourished under the system of free grazing, but larger areas of land were required. James Drummond Jr secured leasehold also of the neighbouring grants owned by Yule (to be known later as 'Woodendale') as well as the Leake and Norman estates including 'Nunyle'.

In 1841 he employed a Scottish shepherd named Ewen Mackintosh. In the following years he engaged Thomas Davis the blacksmith (who had arrived in the *Parmelia* with his family). Davis' daughter Charlotte, who was married to John Herbert, lived in a cottage on Leake's grant known as 'Coondle'.

Other employees at 'Hawthornden' were Henry Green and John Cook, whose wife Jenette (according to her descendants) planted the roses which flourish along the road past the homestead.

'Hawthornden' was a convenient stopping place for colonists on their way up the Toodyay Valley and to the Victoria Plains. Since there was no wayside inn at Toodyay until 1849, people of high and low degree were grateful for the hospitality offered there.

In December 1849 Bishop Short was a notable visitor who conducted a service at Drummond's barn. Almost every person in the district attended. Farm machinery was put aside and bags of grain served as seating for most of the congregation. However as the Bishop was a brother-in-law of Squire Phillips he slept at 'Culham'.

There were no storekeepers or merchants in the district until 1861. Like many other land holders who employed several workers, James Drummond Jr kept enough stock of tea, sugar and clothing for his men as well as for the small farmers who brought their grain to be ground at his mill. Money never changed hands since payment was made by a portion of the grain. He also gave credit to sandalwooders in exchange for their loads. When the price of sandalwood fell suddenly in 1849 he was left with stacks of wood with little value.

However in the 1850s after the introduction of convicts Drummond won valuable contracts for provisioning the Convict Establishment. He required more wheat to mill than he could grow. He then offered small blocks of his uncleared land, rental free, to those who were prepared to clear, fence and grow crops on them. The successful applicants included some newly arrived free immigrants as well as ticket-of-leave men who in time became small farmers on land of their own.

Drummond's horse-drawn mill was incapable of handling all the grain. With the financial backing of George Shenton, a Perth merchant, he imported expensive machinery for a steam mill. The builder of the three-storey mill was George Hasell, an expiree brickmaker who built also 'Vine Cottage' near the mill in preparation for Drummond's marriage in 1856 to Martha Sewell. Hasell became the leading builder at Toodyay after he proved his skill while working on St Stephen's Church.

After James Drummond the botanist died in 1863 followed by his wife in 1864, his son James commissioned Hasell to build a large two-storey home at 'Hawthornden'. His wife Martha quickly moved into this new home. Hasell also built a substantial brick barn and other outbuildings near the homestead, employing two ticket-of-leave men, a brickmaker named John Hinton and James Cook, a carpenter, as well as other labourers. He was already engaged to build the Victoria Hotel and was to receive contracts for many homesteads.

By this time owners of some grants were beginning to fence their land entirely, often closing off the old well-trodden tracks past their doors. This was resented by some neighbours, wayfarers, shepherds and sandalwooders alike. In 1866 James Drummond gave land for a cemetery on part of the 'Mt Anderson' grant near the bridge over the Avon. It was accepted although the grant was mortgaged (possibly to enable Drummond to purchase U3). The road to the cemetery was part of the track past 'Hawthornden' up the Toodyay Valley. In 1872 he gave up more land for an official road to Bolgart and thence to the Victoria Plains and New Norcia.

Since Drummond was Chairman of both the Toodyay and Victoria Plains Road Boards after their inception in 1871 he could facilitate these moves. He had large pastoral leases along the Moore River and saw the advantage of good roads to isolated regions. In 1870 and 1872 disastrous floods at Toodyay and the Victoria Plains ruined crops and washed away buildings, including the cottage occupied by his miller, Charles Marris. Then the markets for wool, sandalwood and horses all fell at the same time leaving Drummond, like many other landholders, deeply in debt to the merchants. However James Drummond continued to give credit to

Drummond's Steam Mill built 1856 with additions on both sides made early 1900s. The place suffered many floods.

Mill stones recovered from the Brook. Photograph 1962.

Drummond cemetery. Photograph: Robyn Taylor 2004.

IN MEMORY OF

JAMES DRUMMOND	JAMES DRUMMOND Junior
d. 26·3·1863	d. 8·2·1873
SARAH DRUMMOND	MICHAEL CLARKSON
d. 12·6·1864	d. 1871
JOHNSON DRUMMOND	EDWARD ELLIS CLARKSON
d. 1845	1844 – 1865
JANE MACKINTOSH	INFANT DESCENDANT OF
1777 – 1874	J. DRUMMOND Jnr.

BELIEVED BURIED HERE

The Memorial Tablet. Photograph: Robyn Taylor 2004.

customers who came to his mill and store, confident that he could recover financially when seasons and markets were favourable.

The lush growth of pastures in 1873 created fire hazards. After three days fighting a bush fire which threatened 'Hawthornden', James Drummond died of exhaustion and pneumonia. His will gave evidence of his wealth during the good years, for he owned several properties and large leaseholds in different parts of the colony. But he had directed in the will for his executors to sell these and distribute the proceeds among his heirs. The trustees were obliged to sell on a falling market when creditors demanded payment.

By 1874 the 'Steam Mill' and 'Vine Cottage' were bought by the Dempster brothers, while 'Hawthornden' and 'Mt Anderson' were bought by Connor who secured also the lease of 'Coondle'. Several Perth merchants (who were among the creditors) out of sympathy for Drummond's widow, organised the purchase of an annuity to assist her to rear her family. She left 'Hawthornden' to live with relatives at York in a home equally as comfortable and accommodating.

Drummond's place as a community leader was filled by Squire Phillips who was absent from 'Culham' for long periods and lacked the foresight, wisdom and selflessness of Drummond.

Connor did not occupy 'Hawthornden', but engaged John Macpherson who had been living at 'Coondle' to manage the property. They occupied the main cottage beside the two-storey homestead. Each day Macpherson's daughter took a pannican of fresh milk to the workmen on the estate. One of them, an expiree, in January 1889 made improper advances to the girl and was promptly dismissed. That night he took his revenge. After the family had gone to bed he stole in and bludgeoned the parents to death and almost killed a son. The daughter climbed through a window and fled for help. The murderer was found a few days later in bushland. Stories were told of these tragedies for generations to come.

The Dempsters in 1886 sold the 'Steam Mill' and 'Vine Cottage' to a Northam merchant George Throssell. He sold it in 1902 to Quigley and Slee, millers from York who thought to profit from the sales of farm land at Bolgart. They installed new machinery and did fairly well until a flood in 1915 damaged the mill beyond repair.

After Connor died in 1898 'Hawthornden' was bought by W.G. Hawkes, a noted South Australian breeder of stud sheep at Koonoona. Hawkes engaged Vincent Klem as the manager in charge.

Sir Ernest Lee Steere bought 'Hawthornden' in 1915 and made extensive alterations to the homestead. His son Ernest, who inherited the property, restored several of the old farm buildings erected by the ticket-of-leave men. These were recognised as of heritage value by the National Trust. The burial ground near the home in which so many Drummonds were buried was re-fenced and the headstones restored with the aid of donations from descendants. This historic cemetery was then cared for by the Lee Steere family. Among those buried there are James Drummond Jr, James Drummond the botanist and his wife and her sister Miss Jane Mackintosh (who came to the colony in her declining years), the two men killed by Aborigines (Johnston Drummond and Edward Ellis Clarkson) as well as Michael Clarkson and possibly the two-year-old daughters of James Drummond Jr and his sister Euphemia Mackintosh.

References
Interviews with descendants of Drummond, Harper, Macpherson, Marris, Davis, Cook and Klein, undertaken by Rica Erickson.

24. BARN ELMS

'Barn Elms' (Avon Location 54 of 1610 acres) was selected by Thomas Waters (1794-1864) who arrived in the colony in 1829. He was the son of a widow who ran a grog shop at Barn Elms near London. He qualified for a free grant, part of which he selected near Guildford and named 'Olive Farm' where he grew a vineyard and vegetables. The rest of his grant was selected in the Toodyay Valley in 1836. The freehold title to this land was obtained in 1842 after his brother Robert (1813-1893) performed the location duties.

When Robert arrived in 1833 he was nineteen years younger than Thomas who may have hoped that Robert would occupy the Toodyay land and thus secure freehold title for him. But Robert preferred the more civilised life at Guildford. Moreover he was courting Susan Betts and it may be that he was bargaining with Thomas for a share of the Toodyay grant.

In 1842 he won a contract for the weekly delivery of mail from York to 'Katrine'. He married Susan in February and they moved to Toodyay where they could live with her brother Charles Betts and his wife. Betts was leasing Location 15 which was within walking distance of the Waters' grant, and Robert could perform the location duties by clearing some of it and possibly pasturing Betts' stock on it. There was no cottage on it until after his first child Robert Betts Waters was born at Toodyay in July 1842.

During that year Robert Waters completed the Location duties on Thomas' grant and he asked the surveyor to mark clearly on the map the boundary between his own and his brother's half. He named his 'Barn Elms', while Thomas' half became known later as 'Brooklyn'.

Robert grew vines and specialised in growing potatoes for which there was a good return for most of the year. He also pruned the vines grown on most of the homesteads of the district. He had no need for much of his land so most of Avon Location 54 was leased to the Ferguson family. They were brought to the colony by T.N. Yule in 1841 but moved to the Toodyay Valley in the late 1840s. The eldest son Thomas Ferguson remained at Guildford while son James farmed their lease at 'Barn Elms'. Their aging father Alexander Ferguson set up his blacksmithy in a mud hut beside a ford at the Toodyay Brook. He made a good living because many men were moving stock to the pastures along the Moore

River or to distant sandalwood country. In 1847 the Gregory brothers, who were heading north to explore the land as far as the Irwin River, had their horses shod by old Alex Ferguson. Another notable customer was Dom Salvado, the Benedictine missionary at New Norcia. He came to Ferguson's smithy loaded with plough-shares carried on his back, to have them sharpened. Today a grassy mound is all that survives of this historic building. By 1851 the traffic through 'Barn Elms' encouraged Robert Waters to apply for a licence for a wayside inn. His home had six rooms which he declared was big enough to provide accommodation for wayfarers as well as his family of six children. The Resident Magistrate J.S. Harris opposed this move saying there were two inns at Toodyay, only a few miles away, and already he had too many drunken brawlers to control.

Waters' application was favoured by S.P. Phillips, a very influential owner of a large property further up the Valley. Waters was granted his licence on condition that he would enlarge his premises. After Phillips sailed to England on a very lengthy visit, Harris revoked Waters' licence, saying that he was too dilatory in adding rooms to his house.

The floods of 1859 and 1860 may have damaged Waters' house. In 1861 he bought 100 acres (Location 279) which included a spring. This was the ideal size for growing potatoes and vegetables. Some bricks were fired in 1859 by James Riley for the building of the fireplace, mud bats were made for the walls. Timber and shelves were stripped from the first home.

Robert Waters' eldest son, named Robert Betts Waters, married Mary Ann Ferguson in 1863 and was leasing 'Brooklyn' from his uncle Thomas at Guildford. Young Robert was a strict teetotaller in stark contrast to his father Robert, who had become an alcoholic. His uncle Thomas Waters at Guildford also frowned upon excessive drinking. Relatives said that if Robert Betts Waters had played his cards better he could have owned 'Brooklyn' which old Thomas had bequeathed to his daughter, but she was out of favour with her father because she married a profligate expiree. However Thomas Waters died in 1869 without changing his will.

In his old age Robert Waters' wife tolerated her husband's weakness for alcohol and when he began drinking heavily at one of the inns at Toodyay she left him there in peace for a day or two before bringing him home. They were a jovial couple and very popular with their children and grandchildren. The old man made 'Jumping Jack' toys that could dance. Some of these grandchildren passed their door on the way to school and often were enticed to stay the day, playing games and yarning with the aging couple. Both died in 1893 within a short time of each other. Their sons and daughters found marriage partners in the neighbouring families of Ferguson, Cook, Lloyd, Lee and Rumble, whose descendants treasure many stories about their jolly old ancestors.

References
Interviews with several descendants by Rica Erickson.

Waters' papers in the hands of the Schorer family.

Letter from Mrs Waters in England, March 1849, advising Robert not to return to London, which he was thinking of doing during the economic depression of the 1840s. Copy held by Rica Erickson.

25. COONDLE ESTATE

The Coondle Estate (Avon Location 1 of 7000 acres) was granted to George Leake after his exploration of the Toodyay Valley in 1836 with George Fletcher Moore. None of the Leake family lived on the property. The first of the lessees was J.C. Mackie who may have built a cottage on it and performed the necessary location duties for Leake.

Ruins of John Macpherson's house at Coondle.
Photograph 1962.

The second to lease 'Coondle' was James Drummond Jr whose employees lived in the cottage. One of these was John Herbert who in 1847 went sandalwooding and then moved to the Toodyay townsite. The next to occupy the cottage was Ewen Mackintosh who married Drummond's sister and in 1854 bought one-third of Yule's grant which he named 'Glendearg'. Mackintosh's cousin John Macpherson was a lessee at 'Coondle' for about 20 years. He built a substantial stone house in 1865 employing two ticket-of-leave men, Peter Brehart, a stone mason and John Bolyne, a carpenter. Both these men were to build other large homes in the district.

A series of dry years and low prices followed and by 1868 Macpherson was in debt. His assets were auctioned at a Sheriff's sale, which enabled him to continue leasing 'Coondle' for another ten years. In 1878 he faced the same situation and accepted Daniel Connor's offer of employment as farm manager at 'Hawthornden'.

Parts of 'Coondle' were leased to the Dempster brothers and others such as Charles Ferguson, who was the occupant of the stone house when it was struck by lightning and deemed uninhabitable. The stone walls were still standing in the year 2003.

In 1898 'Coondle' was bought by the Government and subdivided as farmlets of fifteen to 410 acres. This was in response to public demand to open up huge grants and pastoral leases more suited for farming than pastoral use. The heavily populated Goldfields area offered good markets for farm produce. The advertisements stated that 'Coondle' was eminently suitable for orchards, vineyards, dairying and pig and poultry farms. Also vegetables could be grown by irrigation from the Toodyay Brook.

Old settlers were scornful of this claim, knowing that the Brook had only a few pools of water in the summer months. Charles Ferguson's cousin Hannah Fawell and her husband came from the Swan district and bought a block near Dewars Pool where they planted an orchard and grew vegetables for sale from their door. After John Fawell died Hannah conducted a telephone exchange at her small store. This served the Bindoon Road small farmers including Cook, Waters, McCluney, Lee, Rumble and O'Neill and Britt. Most of them were former employees of Squire Phillips of 'Culham'. Britt and Phillips would have been acquainted in England where Squire Phillips' father owned Blewberry Manor and Britt's father owned Blewberry Inn.

The road from Bindoon to Toodyay led past Britt's house to a bridge that crossed the Toodyay Brook. This was used during the winter months when the Bindoon settlers' road to Perth was impassable over swampy land. They then conducted their business at Toodyay instead and brought their wheat to Drummond's 'Steam Mill'. They usually called at Britt's home.

In 1857 John Britt's wife received a legacy from England. They decided to build a neat two-storey inn and a separate brewing room around which they planted prickly roses to deter thieves. A ticket-of-leave plasterer named John Smith worked with them for a year after the bricklaying was finished. After all this labour Britt's application for an inn licence was refused. Undeterred he converted the brewing room into a flourmill which was operated by a small steam engine until the expensive sifting silks wore out.

Towards the end of the century John Britt and his neighbours along the Bindoon Road built a mud bat schoolhouse near the bridge to accommodate the growing number of school children. It was so hot in summer they called it the Black Hole of Calcutta and were pleased when a hall was built at 'Coondle' which could be used instead. This community centre soon included tennis courts and a cement cricket pitch laid down by Morgan Ford, the builder of several mud brick cottages at 'Coondle', one of which in 2000 was still intact, to be seen near the railway siding.

Morgan Ford employed local tradesmen such as Henry (son of John) Hasell as his bricklayer and plasterer, Thomas Martin as the carpenter (possibly the expiree) and Judd Towler, the Bejoording maker of mud bats.

A large ramjam or pise building near the roadside was built for the Vetter family from France who planted a vineyard and proposed to make wine. This building was to be their living quarters and winery until a permanent home could be built. Baptiste Achilles Vetter was born near Lyons in France in 1827 and came to Australia with his wife and daughter Gabrielle about 1896. This move was encouraged by their sons who were prospectors on the Goldfields and owned a hotel and a mine known at 'Vettersburg' near Bardoc and Coolgardie. They could speak English but their parents and Gabrielle could not, so one of them, named Victor, managed their business by correspondence.

At first Gabrielle bought four or five acres, a few miles from Pinjarra where they grew vegetables and poultry for a living while the brothers decided upon the place they could all live together after the sale of their goldfields property. They bought 'Coondle' Lots 37, 38 and 12, one of which was in Gabrielle's name. While the winery was being built Charles Ferguson was paid to plough the ground. They then planted vine cuttings.

The walls of the winery were up by September 1898. By November the rafters were added by William Perl (Peril) and on New Years Day 1899 the roof was complete. All the purchasing of materials and the building contracts were handled by correspondence by Victor in addition to letters sent to another French family in Perth. The Vetters first vintage yielded 20 gallons of wine, mainly through the industry of Gabrielle.

Old Vetter died in 1900 and his wife died four years later. Gabrielle carried on alone until her brother Victor sent his wife and children to 'Coondle'. He wound up his affairs on the goldfields but was uncertain whether to buy more land at 'Coondle' from Kingston and Leeder or to lease a larger area at Moore River. In the meantime he leased their 'Coondle' land to Ferguson who allowed his pigs to break into the

Vetters Winery.
Photograph 1962.

Vettersburgh Hotel, 1890s
on the Goldfields.
Source: J. S. Battye,
Cyclopedia of Western
Australia, Vol. 2, 1913.

vineyard and damage the vines. After that Gabrielle left for France. A neighbour at Coondle leased her property and Victor went into business in Perth.

Vetter's pise winery was still standing in the 1960s, but after the iron roofing was removed, the mud walls began to deteriorate. Finally the ruins were demolished when a wheat silo was built on the site. After that many of the 'Coondle' blocks changed hands and the newcomers had no knowledge of Vetter nor of the winery they built.

A more enduring memory is that of another foreign settler, Charles Soong Yock Lunn, who bought David Lloyd's eighty-acre block. He spoke English fluently and is reputed to have acted on behalf of other Chinese in the Consul's office in Perth.

Yock Lunn was born in Canton in 1871 and came to Western Australia in September 1899. His wife Wee Shin Yock Lunn also came from Canton where she was born in 1880. She followed her husband in 1900 and bore him a son. Yock Lunn planted ten acres of oranges on his 80-acre block and grew vegetables on a large scale on the remaining land, using water in summer from a pool in the Brook. He sent his produce by train to the lucrative markets at Kalgoorlie and on one occasion sent a trainload of cauliflowers. After this the locals called him the 'Cauliflower King'. His siding was then known as 'Lunn's Landing'.

When motorcars replaced horses, settlers found it easier and faster to drive to Toodyay for business and pleasure. A school bus took the children to town for their education. In 1939 the 'Coondle' hall was bought by the Toodyay branch of the Country Women's Association and rebuilt to serve as their Rest Room in town.

The small farm lots were being amalgamated to make viable farms of bigger acreages. However by the year 2000 this trend was reversed. Towns-people seeking a rural environment wanted these small lots of land. The 1898 surveys facilitated the sales of land. Modern homes were built on the small farmlets and 'Coondle' became a suburb of Toodyay.

References
Copies of Britt and Vetter letters etc. held by Rica Erickson.
Reminiscences of descendants of early settlers.

26. CULHAM

'Culham' (Avon Location 4 of 12,513 acres) was granted originally to Dr Waylen. In 1839 he sold it at half a crown an acre to Samuel Pole Phillips and Edward Hamersley who were related by marriage. Hamersley had arrived in the colony in 1839 and was buying several grants of land from needy colonists, planning to lease them and to live on the rentals like landed gentry in England. He was already comfortably settled in his home at 'Pyrton' near Guildford. Phillips was on his way to study for the ministry under Bishop Short at Adelaide when his ship called at Fremantle in May 1839.

'Culham'.
Photograph: Robyn Taylor
2003.

'Culham'. First cottage
(centre) with second cottage
on left and the two-storey
home on the right, 1856.
Source: P.W.H. Thiel &
Co., Twentieth Century
Impressions of WA, *1901.*

The youngest sons of English gentry usually adopted a career in the ministry, but Phillips lacked enthusiasm for becoming a clergyman. He was very knowledgeable about horses and when Hamersley suggested forming a partnership in horsebreeding in Western Australia Phillips readily agreed. Moves were afoot to open a trade in India for horses. Hamersley had a shrewd head for business and could manage the sales from his home at Guildford while it was agreed Phillips could go to Waylen's land and undertake the breeding of suitable horses. A cottage was already there known as the 'Shepherds Hut'. He named their property 'Culham', after his ancestral home in England. In April 1840 he advertised that he would be taking horses to 'Culham' and was prepared to accept more from those interested in breeding.

Since none of the grants were fenced stock were left to range freely in the bush. In August Samuel Moore of Guildford sent some colts to 'Culham' for agistment and was very concerned to hear they were missing for seven weeks at distant waterholes. Phillips was building stables and yards at 'Culham' and by October 1840 advertised in *The Inquirer* that his stallion Noble was available for service.

One of Phillips' neighbours, T.N. Yule, formerly an officer in the India Army, had plans to sell horses in India, but a worldwide trade recession in the mid-1840s kept these plans in abeyance. Also, there was a limited clientele in the colony. In 1843 Hamersley and Phillips sailed to England and 'Culham' was left to the management of John York. Phillips returned in 1845 and York moved to Gingin where he bought a small block of land. In 1847 Phillips married Sophie Roe, the eldest daughter of the Surveyor General.

Mrs Roe had six other daughters whose marriages would have to be arranged satisfactorily. She approved of Phillips as a son-in-law because a younger man with inferior prospects was also courting Sophie. A new house was built at 'Culham' of more spacious proportions than the Shepherds Hut. It was built of mud brick beside the Toodyay Brook where suitable clay was found. The Hut could then be occupied by the next farm manager Thomas O'Neill.

Phillips and his wife Sophie sailed to Adelaide with the Roe family in January 1850 to be present at the wedding of her sister Matilda to a South Australian pastoralist named Philip Butler. The ceremony was performed by Bishop Short. The Phillips were his guest for some of their stay at Adelaide. They did not return to 'Culham' until October.

During this long absence O'Neill was left to manage the property. He advanced his plans to become an independent farmer like Joseph York who held a pastoral lease at his small farm in the Swan district and was prospering. O'Neill leased an area around Wattening Spring with pre-emptive right of purchasing the land around the Spring. This was some miles north from 'Culham' and he could graze stock there without competing against Phillips or others whose stock grazed freely to the west of 'Culham'.

When Hamersley returned to the colony in January 1850 he probably had prior knowledge of the proposal to send convicts to the colony and saw the possibility of winning contracts for supplying meat to the Convict Establishment. In 1851 he and Phillips dissolved their horsebreeding partnership and formed the Cattle Company including L.C. Burges and B.U. Vigors. Hamersley then leased his half of the Toodyay grant to Phillips. Phillips had already explored the Irwin Valley and the Cattle Company leased the whole area. Burges as manager of this lease built a house on the lower reaches of the Irwin River and named it Irwin House.

The India market for horses was promising so Phillips continued breeding them at 'Culham' on a larger scale. He needed financial aid as well as a partner for management. In 1853 he sailed to England accompanied by Sophie, their baby Fanny and Sophie's sister Emma Roe. Another child was born before their return in June 1855. They were accompanied by James Guy Thomson as a partner and young Augustus Lee Steere who had some capital and hoped to be included in the partnership.

The newcomers each paid Phillips £100 for gaining experience in farming and pastoral methods in the colony. They also spent a lot of time on the road between 'Culham' and Perth bringing up stores and materials required for building a new brick two-storeyed home alongside the mud brick house. Several men of the bond class were employed. George Hasell the brickmaker was the contractor, George Brown and Wright were the carpenters and Alex Fagan was the stonemason.

In 1857 Mrs Phillips held a grand housewarming party entertaining several eminent guests from Perth as well as friends in the district. It was about this time that Phillips became known as 'The Squire' and Thomson as 'Gentleman'. The partnership between the two men was more closely knit after Thomson married Emma Roe in 1856.

The newly weds took up residence in Captain Scully's cottage at Bolgart, beside the Water Reserve. The cottage had been recently vacated by Edward E. Beere and his large family. Beere was a Dublin lawyer, son of a lawyer who leased a mansion there known as 'Anneville'. Both lawyers accumulated huge debts and Beere came to the colony hoping to make a fresh start.

After vacating Scully's cottage he leased land to the west which Phillips used in the 1840s as a free run. There he took out a tillage lease. By making the necessary improvements and the regular payment of licence fees he could within a few years receive freehold title. He named this home Anneville and hired ticket-of-leave men to build it and to fence and clear the land. When short of credit he borrowed money from Phillips.

By then Phillips held undisputed leases of hundreds of thousands of acres of pastoral land with water at Wattening and Bolgart and had no rivals to the north beyond Wyening Springs.

In March 1858 the partners won a valuable contract to deliver a hundred or more horses to India. An advertisement was placed in a Perth newspaper inviting other horsebreeders to help fill the order. Phillips took charge of loading 138 on board the *Caduceus*, a very risky matter. The horses were taken by barge, a few at a time to the anchored ship and each was transferred in a sling on board. Only one horse was lost – when the sling broke.

Phillips and Thomson were both domineering and hasty tempered. They had quarreled in the past and in August 1858 Thomson took his wife to Perth and the partnership ended. The dispute may have been Phillips' wish to add Lee Steere to their business. Thomson stayed some months in Perth before deciding to settle in the Blackwood district. The wives maintained a loving relationship but the breach between the two men was never healed.

In the same year as Thomson left Bolgart, Phillips and Lee Steere bought a freehold block at Wyening, and after hard bargaining with O'Neill he agreed to waive his pre-emptive right to the land around Wattening Spring. The Lee Steeres planned to build a house somewhere near 'Culham'.

During the next seven years Phillips spent a lot of time away from 'Culham', usually on Cattle Company business in partnership with Edward Hamersley. Several small freehold blocks of land in the Irwin district had to be bought to prevent small farmers from buying this land around the springs and wells. Then Phillips and Burges, the manager at 'Irwin House', offered agistment to other pastoralists. Robert de Burgh sent a large herd of cattle for fattening at the Irwin, but the mob, when turned loose, headed back to home and perished in poison country. Robert de Burgh was awarded damages.

In January 1860 Burges sailed for a holiday in Ireland and did not return until November 1862. Phillips managed the Irwin lease for a year after which Hamersley gave him the management in Perth of the Cattle Company's sales of stock. Phillips and his family then lived in Perth.

When he learnt that Hamersley had paid the new manager at Irwin a salary Phillips was angry and asked for payment for his past services. He threatened to return to the Irwin and to hold the Company's financial records as his sole possession, but Hamersley was unperturbed. Phillips owed the Company for the damages claimed by de Burgh. He cleared the debt by selling some of his shares in the Company to Colonel Bruce and then returned to 'Culham'.

There he encountered another problem. Beere owed him one hundred pounds. The two men arranged for Phillips to receive Beere's freehold title but allowing Beere to remain at 'Anneville' for twenty one years free of charge. To their dismay when the surveyor came to define the boundaries he found that 'Anneville' was built on a neighbour's pastoral lease. Both Phillips and Beere were left inconsolate.

Squire Phillips was always a spendthrift when he received an occasional legacy from England. In 1865 he took his family to pay a lengthy visit to relatives in Adelaide. There the Squire gained praise and a medal from the Royal Humane Society for his bravery when he rescued some people from drowning by riding his horse into dangerous surf to bring them safely to shore.

Dissension continued between Phillips and Hamersley respecting the Squire's handling of business. The partnership was dissolved in 1867. The Irwin Valley leases were divided among them with Phillips receiving his third portion at Mingenew. In the future this was to be managed by his eldest son Samuel.

Hamersley's lease of his half of 'Culham' to Phillips expired about the same time. He rented it to Walter Padbury instead. It was then known as 'Cowardine' and used as a fattening run for Padbury's cattle in charge of a resident stockman.

During Phillips' absences from 'Culham' O'Neill was in charge of a large staff including several expirees such as O'Dea, Pritchard and Lahiff as well as a Parkhurst lad named William Beard. All these men married immigrant girls and lived in mud brick cottages at 'Culham' until they bought small farm blocks nearby.

In 1871 Squire Phillips and Sophie visited Geraldton going by carriage, accompanied by their livery man the Aboriginal Narrier. Women rarely travelled along this rough road and their transport would be by dray or wagon. So the Phillips' arrival at the isolated homesteads along the way created quite a stir. They were unexpected guests but welcomed, for their hosts were formerly from Toodyay. At each step Sophie wrote letters to be sent back to her family at 'Culham' by a mailman that passed through on horseback each week. The most intimate reunion was with the Fanes, their relatives at 'Irwin House'.

A year later heavy floods along the Toodyay Brook washed away several mud bat cottages. Phillips' old cottage survived but the cellar of the two-storey homestead was flooded. This calamity caused Squire

Out buildings at 'Culham', c. 1870.
The old barn is next to the open shed.

An old barn.
Photograph: Robyn Taylor
2003.

Phillips to build a new home on higher ground, incorporating the sturdy old 'Shepherd's Hut'. The new house was single-storeyed because Phillips was plagued by gout and didn't like climbing stairs.

Phillips resigned from the Toodyay Roads Board in 1879 and took his wife on an extended visit to England. His son John Hugh, who was left in charge of 'Culham', regarded this as an improvident move and also may have been diffident about his own election to the Roads Board in 1880 to maintain the family presence there.

Squire Phillips had served on Road Committees since 1840 and was a foundation member of the Toodyay Road Board in 1871. The road to 'Culham' was said to be the best in the colony and he may have had doubts about its maintenance during his absence for he mistrusted the judgement of expirees who were beginning to sway Roads Board policies. Daniel Connor was chairman of the Toodyay Roads Board during the absence of Phillips who resumed chairmanship once more in 1881, but he was voted out of that office in 1883.

John Hugh Phillips married Laura Lukin in 1881. He renovated the mud brick house beside the Brook and replaced the thatched roof with galvanised iron. He took over the management of 'Culham' while Laura assumed Sophie's role as organiser of Church bazaars and teaching

Phillips family gathering at the new home. The Squire has a white beard.
Courtesy: Phillips family collection.

children at Sunday School to read and write as well as to study the Scriptures.

After the railway was built to Toodyay in 1887 the two homesteads at 'Culham' were filled with guests from Perth who were invited to come by train to attend the annual bazaars and the customary cricket matches. Squire Phillips in his old age had not lost his enjoyment of travel. In 1895 when he received a legacy he insisted, despite his gout, upon visiting England once more. Regardless of the expense, as always, he indulged Sophie in her wish to buy a very elegant Paris gown. (Many years later it was donated to the Toodyay Museum.)

As the Squire grew more frail he had a personal attendant named Wakeford, while Sophie handed her housekeeping duties to Kate Mitchell, who in years to come was hostess at Government House when her brother Sir James Mitchell was Lt Governor.

In 1899 the Government granted money for building an Agricultural Hall at the eastern end of 'Culham'. Community activities such as cricket, tennis, football and even horse races were held there as well as public meetings and dances. Social life at the homestead decreased, but to the end of his life his former employees humoured the old Squire by saluting him with a tug of the forelock.

Samuel Pole Phillips died at 'Culham' in 1901. Sophie asked a former employee, William Syred of Bejoording to prepare the body for burial. A year later she was buried beside him in the historic family cemetery of St Philips Church. In his life time Squire Phillips had been a nominee member of the Legislative Council 1857-1872, and long-time member of the Toodyay, Northam and Victoria Plains Agricultural Society formed in 1854. He served on the local Board of Education as well as the Road Board. The old Squire and his wife lived to see the beginning of a new century and the Federation of the colonies. Their passing marked the end of the old colonial ways which had been maintained for so long at 'Culham'.

References

Mary Albertus Bain, *Ancient Landmarks*, UWA Press, Nedlands, 1975.

Samuel Moore's diaries, copied by favour of a descendant Joanna Seabrook.

Sophie Phillips' diaries, Battye Library. WAA. HS. 458.

Robert Stephens, 'Mingenew Story', in *Early Days*, Journal of the Royal W.A. Historical Society.

London Illustrated News, 1856.

Letter from Marjorie Stanisford-Smith, granddaughter of J.G. Thomson.

Minutes of Toodyay Road Board, Battye Library. WAA. 762.

Minutes of Toodyay, Northam and Victoria Plains Agricultural Society, Battye Library. WAA 627.

Interviews with Mrs J.C. Phillips, Mrs H.W. Clarkson nee Phillips, Mrs Samuel Evans Burges of 'Collingully' and descendants of Britt, Beard, Edmonds, McCluney, O'Neill, Pritchard and Syred.

27. THE ANGLICAN CHURCH OF ST PHILIP

The Anglican Church of St Philip was also known as the Toodyay Valley Church. Materials for the building were assembled in 1849 after Squire Phillips and his wife returned from a lengthy visit to Adelaide where his brother-in-law, Bishop Short resided. Donations for the building were solicited in England and Australia. John Britt sawed the timber from the Bindoon forest, stone was carted to the site and galvanised iron recently imported from England was ordered in 1847.

By February 1853 Archdeacon Wollaston reported to Bishop Short that 'a very neat substantial stone church has just been erected, consisting of a nave and a small porch'. The Phillips were unable to attend the first service scheduled for May 1853, having sailed for England on a lengthy holiday. Just after they left 'Culham' a severe storm damaged the church roof. Rev. Harper and his parishioners worked hard to bring the building to some semblance of order in time for the opening. Rev. Pownall who preached the first sermon announced that the collection would be devoted to ordering suitable fittings for the interior.

The first marriage in St Philips Church was conducted by Rev. Harper in February 1854, when Drummond's shepherd John Henry Johnson was wed to Mary Dunroche, an immigrant servant girl.

The church was in an isolated place and there was no caretaker. Wayfarers used the porch as a convenient camping place. When Rev. Wollaston next visited St Philips Church he expressed his distress in a forceful letter to Rev. Pownall. Among the trespassers were John Cousins and his family who were walking from 'Buckland' near Northam to find work at 'Glendearg' in the Toodyay Valley.

After the Phillips returned to 'Culham' in June 1855 they built a fine new house before beginning work on the church which was finally completed in 1857. Money for the renovations was raised at a bazaar in Toodyay conducted by Mrs Phillips who brought trinkets from England. To celebrate the first service in the newly furnished church she invited a large number of guests to dine at her new home.

Rev. Harper regularly officiated at the Toodyay Valley Church until his death in 1872. The next service was held in 1874 after the appointment of Rev. W.H. Pidcock. Under his guidance renovations were made to the church in 1876. Funds were raised at tea meetings and bazaars. Numerous

*St Philip's Church, Culham.
Photograph Robyn Taylor
2002.*

'sewing bees' to make garments and other items for sale at bazaars were held at the homes of Mrs Phillips of 'Culham' and Mrs Mackintosh of 'Glendearg'. Those held at 'Culham' were pleasant social occasions but those at 'Glendearg' were remembered as rather solemn occasions.

Sundays were also solemn. Although sport on that day of the week was frowned upon, the families who gathered for the church service enjoyed meeting their neighbours and it became customary to have a picnic lunch. The men sometimes played cricket and carefully hid the bat before the Squire and his family arrived. There was some trepidation when he came early one Sunday and they feared the treasured bat would be confiscated. They were very relieved when the Squire said they could play after the service and later presented them with a new bat. He enjoyed keeping them in suspense and was notorious for his practical jokes.

Rev. T.H. Friel who succeeded Rev. Pidcock served the parish during 1888 to 1894. He was concerned that the little church had not been consecrated. Energies were directed towards making repairs and re-roofing the building. The long-delayed consecration ceremony was performed by Bishop Riley in September 1895 before a congregation of 200 people.

By then several burials had taken place at the church cemetery, the first being in 1860 of the Squire's two-year-old son, Newton. During the next century there was little space left for more graves. Burials were then limited to those who were descendants of the original parishioners. The headstones reveal much of their histories.

References

Wollaston's Albany Journals 1848-1856, Collected by Rev. Canon A. Burton, Paterson Brokensha Ltd, Perth, 1954.

Mrs Phillips diaries, copies in Battye Library and Mitchell Library (NSW).

Interviews with descendants of Britt, Cook, Syred, Ralph, Waters, McCluney, Macpherson and Kilpin.

28. HASELEY

'Haseley' is the eastern half of Location 4 originally owned jointly by S.P. Phillips and Edward Hamersley. When the partnership was dissolved in 1851 Phillips held a fourteen-year lease of Hamersley's half until 1867, after which it was leased to Walter Padbury and known as 'Cowardine'. Padbury sent cattle there to be fattened. His stockman lived in a hut around which a few acres were cleared. The last man in charge was Patrick Hennessey employed in 1884. He had arrived in the colony with his family in 1883 and moved to Goomalling in 1891.

'Haseley'.
Photograph: Robyn Taylor 2003.

The Haseley Crest.
Courtesy of Hamersley family.

'Haseley', c.1900.
Courtesy Shire of
Toodyay.

Edward Hamersley bequeathed 'Cowardine' to his son Samuel who was on the family property at York. Samuel's son Vernon was sent to England to study at Oxford and Downton Agricultural College. On his return to Western Australia he worked for his father replacing Hennessey when he left 'Cowardine'. The sudden demand for the growing population on the Goldfields encouraged Vernon to clear large areas for cropping and also to buy more land.

Vernon Hamersley married Clara Hicks in 1895, a year before his father's death. He built a modern brick house at 'Cowardine' and renamed the property 'Haseley'. Included in his inheritance was the treasured trophy shaped like a wool bale which his father won in 1875 for realizing the highest price at the first wool sales by public auction to be held in the colony.

This first sale of wool in Perth was a memorable occasion because pastoralists then knew immediately the prices received for their clips instead of waiting for months for the returns after their sale in England. The auctioneer marked the event by offering this trophy to the man who topped the first Western Australian wool sales.

Vernon established his own stud flock. He became President of the Merino Stud Sheep Breeders Association and the annual sales held at 'Haseley' attracted keen buyers. The homestead was enlarged in 1908 by a local builder, Henry Davey. For generations to come, visitors to the annual sales admired the gardens as much as the sheep.

Vernon Hamersley's public career included service on the Toodyay Road Board and other organisations. He was a Member of the Legislative Council from 1904 until his death in 1946. His son Preston carried on the family tradition as excellent flockmasters. After Preston's death his properties were divided among his sons.

References
Daphne Foulkes Taylor, *Hamersley*, Epress Print, 1996.

A.T. Thomas, *A History of Toodyay*, The Toodyay Road Board, 1949.

Christopher Fyfe, *The Balefillers, Western Australian Wool 1826-1896*, UWA Press, Nedlands, 1983.

Above left: 'Haseley' stud sheep sale, 1988. Courtesy Hamersley family.
Above right: Silver cup awarded 1875 for realising the highest price in the first wool sale by public auction in Western Australia. Courtesy Hamersley family.

29. THE BYEEN

'The Byeen' is one-third of the original grant Avon Location 5 of 14,223 acres which was selected by Thomas Newte Yule in 1836 on behalf of his partners Captain Richmond Houghton and Lt. Ninian Lowis. The three men served in the Indian Army and Lowis was connected by marriage with Governor Stirling. As soon as they knew of plans to settle the Swan River Colony the men pooled their resources to buy livestock, machinery, farm tools, seeds, provisions and a sturdy marquee. Lowis wrote to England asking a relative to engage farm labourers and indentured servants to be sent to Fremantle where he or Yule would meet them. Yule's other servants would accompany them from India. It was agreed that Yule would manage their affairs in the colony and that Lowis and Houghton would in turn come from India while on furlough to help him.

'The Byeen'.
Photograph: Robyn Taylor
2002.

'The Byeen', c.1895.
Courtesy Shire of Toodyay.

Yule and Lowis arrived in May 1830. In February 1831 Lowis' servants including Alex Ferguson and his family came from England. The partners qualified for 29,000 acres as a result, but were unable to select this amount along the Swan. So until their selection of land could be finalized they leased R. H. Bland's Swan grant and by occupying it

110

performed location duties. This grant was mortgaged to them by Bland about the time he moved to the York district. By 1836 half of Bland's grant was owned by the partners and named 'Houghton'.

Long before this, Lowis had returned to India having overstayed his leave. Yule was then left to select the 29,000 acres due to the partners and he investigated areas at York, Beverley, Hotham, Plantagenet and the Canning district. In 1836 when he heard of the rich land at Toodyay he selected 15,000 acres there. It occupied about one-third of the whole Valley stretching from Bejoording northwards to beyond the Bolgart Water Reserve that was near his eastern boundary. In addition there was an excellent spring centrally located on their grant. The place came to be known as 'The Byeen', referring to the remarkable balancing rock nearby. (The Aboriginal word for 'the place of the rock'.)

Yule was a widower whose young daughter Elizabeth was in England. In 1837 he married Lucy Harris the daughter of his neighbour Dr Harris of Strelley. Lucy died a year later and their son was reared by the Harris family.

Yule offered one-third of 'The Byeen' to anyone prepared to perform the location duties. However, the water resources on that portion was limited. Dr S.W. Viveash inspected the grant but withdrew from negotiations when he found only a small spring on the land offered to him.

The next to view 'The Byeen' was Captain John Scully who solved the lack of water by the purchase of 160 acres (Avon Location 37) adjacent to the Bolgart Water Reserve near the land which was offered to him. The documents were signed on 11 March 1840 in the presence of the Attorney General G. F. Moore. A shepherd was placed at 'The Byeen' in charge of 800 sheep and Scully proceeded to build a mud brick cottage and outbuilding on his farm block by the Bolgart Reserve.

Lowis had drowned near Singapore in 1838, and some time had lapsed before Yule heard of the accident. It then took Yule even more time to arrange his affairs at Swan River and secure a passage to India in 1841 to settle affairs with Houghton. By then the prospects at Swan River Colony were bleak and Houghton withdrew from the partnership. Yule was unable to return to the colony until January 1842 and by then his employees had completed their indentures. James Miller owned a small farm while Ferguson had a good business as a blacksmith in the same district. In the mid-1840s Yule went to live at 'The Byeen'.

In 1843 Yule was appointed as a Magistrate at York, but spent as much time as possible at Guildford with the Harris family, enjoying the social life there. As a member of the Legislative Council and a Magistrate he often travelled to Perth and York on official business. He was a portly man and found it difficult to mount a horse so he travelled the rough roads in a light two-wheeled vehicle known as a trap. His daughter Elizabeth who came from England in 1841 with the Sewell family was his housekeeper at 'The Byeen' and found life there very monotonous.

By the late-1840s 'The Byeen' was a well-established farm with barns, stables and stockyards near a neat three-roomed stone cottage with gardens. Prospects were brighter following the development of the sandalwood trade. Yule had a good stack of it waiting to be carted with his wool to Guildford during the summer months. In January 1849 a raging bushfire spread through his property. Everything went up in flames except the cottage and the kitchen garden by the spring. His flocks were spared because his shepherds Isaac Doust and Duncan Macpherson were further afield.

Thoroughly disheartened Yule leased 'The Byeen' to Macpherson. He went to Perth and Elizabeth married Sampson Sewell a year later. The rest of Yule's sojourn in the colony was in the Civil Service. Late in 1854 he sold the southern third of 'The Byeen' to Ewen Mackintosh who named it 'Glendearg'. The boundaries were surveyed in 1856. The northern third of Location 5 became known as 'The Carroll'. The name 'The Byeen' was retained for the central third.

Yule retired to England in 1862 leaving his business affairs in the hands of the merchant R. M. Habgood. Duncan Macpherson was a sober, industrious man, but a series of dry years spoilt his crops and a damaging fire left him with no resources. Unable to pay the rental in 1867, his creditors sold all his goods and stock. His brother Donald Macpherson, a pastoralist in the Victoria Plains, assisted Duncan by declaring himself to be one of the creditors and claimed enough of the proceeds of the sale to equip Duncan with stock, machinery and a wagon for him to move to Carnamah where he was the first settler.

Yule died in England in 1868. In 1872 'The Byeen' was sold to James Butterley (1826-1899), a man who came to the colony as a farm labourer and had progressed to become a well-established flockmaster and owned several small blocks around waterholes where he held pastoral leases. Butterley planned to settle all his children on properties of their own, but they had to earn them. His sons managed 'The Byeen' while his daughter Clara at sixteen years of age was their housekeeper. At haymaking and harvest time she cooked for as many as 21 men.

Lucy Butterley at 'The
Byeen'.
Old Gaol Museum,
Shire of Toodyay Collection.

In 1875 Butterley built a large brick house at 'The Byeen'. The contractor was Thomas Davey of York who found Toodyay to be a promising area in which to follow his trade as a builder. The new house was on higher ground than Yule's cottage which was dismantled and rebuilt near the big house to serve as servants' quarters and as a guest house. This was thought to be necessary because the road from Toodyay to Bolgart passed close by Butterley's door. He wished to fence the whole of the grant and to re-route this road along a boundary fence. He was a member of the Road Board, but in 1883 when he asked permission to close the old track, the chairman, Squire Phillips strongly opposed the idea. He had been using that road for forty years and had no desire to lengthen the journey in the future. Other Board Members recalled that in the past the Squire had closed a road through 'Culham'. Phillips was outvoted, losing not only this contest but his dominance in public affairs.

The Butterley family remained in residence until 'The Byeen' was sold to Kenneth Stevenson who came from New Zealand in 1928.

References

A.T. Thomas, *History of Toodyay*, The Toodyay Road Board, 1949.

Rica Erickson, 'Early Days at Bolgart' in *Early Days*, Journal of Royal W.A. Historical Society, Vol. 6, pt 3, p.4 and Vol. 7, pt 3, p.6.

State Records Office. SDUR. 35/461, 22 Nov 1854 regarding the sale of 'The Byeen'.

Battye Library. Correspondence from R. M. Habgood to Absolon.

Lowis' letter to Mangles per favour Dr Pennie Pemberton.

Interviews with Mrs Atwell (Clara's daughter) and K. Stevenson.

30. GLENDEARG

'Glendearg' was the southern third of Location 5 which was bought from Yule in 1854 by Ewen Mackintosh. He came to the colony in 1841 as a shepherd indentured to James Drummond Jr of 'Hawthornden' but soon owned a flock of his own and joined with his cousins the Macphersons to form a company known as the Scotch Shepherds. They secured a large pastoral lease in the Moore River district in 1845.

'Bacton', built in 1923 by G. T. Gooch on the Glendearg grant. Photograph: Robyn Taylor 2003.

'Glendearg' built in 1855 by E. Mackintosh. Source: P.W.H. Thiel & Co., Twentieth Century Impressions, *1901.*

Mackintosh was a gentle giant of a man, industrious and well educated. By 1849 he owned 160 acres (Avon Location 59) at Erandyne Spring. This gave access to pastoral country over which Phillips and Yule's stock had ranged freely. In the same year Mackintosh had the temerity to marry Euphemia Drummond. At first her brothers disapproved of this union of an employee to their sister. The couple occupied a cottage at 'Coondle' for a few years, which was easily arranged because that grant was leased by James Drummond.

By careful management Mackintosh in 1854 had the means to negotiate the purchase of the lower third of Yule's grant and named it 'Glendearg'. In 1856 the boundaries were surveyed and in 1857 the

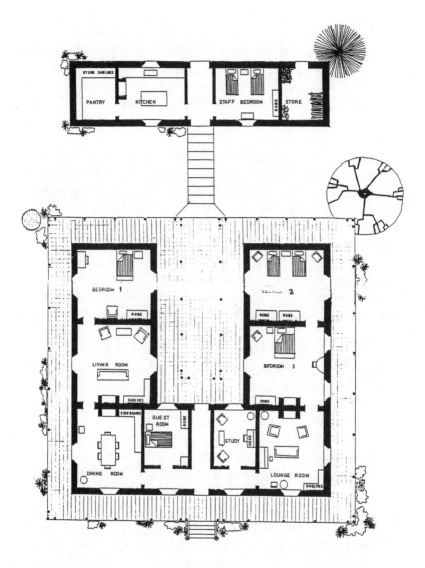

PLAN

Glendearg - Mackintosh home
RESEARCHED & DRAWN
DAVID W. G. THOMAS
DARLINGTON 1972

Scale :-
Date :- 28·1·72
Drawn :- D.Thomas

0   20   40   feet

115

deeds were in his hands. He held large pastoral leases at 'Yulgan' near Bolgart and at 'Noondle' in the Dandaragan district. His sheep were sent to these areas in the care of shepherds, while he concentrated upon the breeding of stud horses and cattle at 'Glendearg'. His wife Euphemia shared his breeding interests and encouraged him to import a valuable bull in 1859. They soon built up a fine herd of dairy cattle. There were several daughters in the family and they shared the chores of milking cows and making butter and cheeses to be sold to privileged customers at Toodyay.

During the year 1863 Mackintosh began building a large brick house, employing two ticket-of-leave men, Robert Baker and Edward Baldock. The hole they dug for making the bricks was to become the cellar, where Euphemia could set the large shallow pans of milk for the cream to rise and where the butter and cheeses could be made and stored.

Ewen Mackintosh and the Drummonds in 1868 combined in a petition for a grant to support a Presbyterian minister in the district. A Congregational minister accepted the appointment. Mackintosh offered land for a church but the small congregation could not raise the funds. Euphemia's family then attended the Anglican Church of St Philip at Culham.

A small government school was conducted in their homestead which was closed when there were not enough pupils. After this some of Mackintosh's daughters attended a private school in Northam and when the 'Glendearg' school was re-opened for a brief period Miss Jane Mackintosh was the teacher.

Euphemia Mackintosh was a stern formidable person. She declared with some pride that she was one of the original pioneers having arrived in the *Parmelia* and claimed also the distinction of never having left the Toodyay district since her arrival with her parents in 1838. Neighbouring women who came to 'Glendearg' to make garments for sale at Church bazaars warned their children to be on their best behaviour. Unlike the enjoyable sewing days at 'Culham' they sewed silently while one of the Mackintosh daughters read aloud an appropriate uplifting story.

Euphemia was one of the first to own a four-wheel carriage which she drove into Newcastle town every week to deliver butter and cheeses. In winter the unpaved streets were very muddy. As her daughters followed her in single file around the puddles some irreverent bystanders likened her to a mother duck followed by her ducklings.

Euphemia reared ten of her eleven children, all of whom were as tall as their father who stood six feet six inches tall and was said to be as broad as three men. The eldest sons, James and Donald who never married, became pastoralists in the Northwest. Two sisters who accompanied them as housekeepers found husbands in that isolated part of the colony.

The five maiden sisters who remained with their mother were notable for their skilful riding and love of horses. When their father died in 1881 the youngest child Robert Ewen (always known as Ewen) was only thirteen years of age and was well spoiled. He accompanied his sisters when they drove their dry milking cows to summer pastures at Dandaragan and became noted for his skill with the stockwhip while selecting a beast from the herd. Ewen, who escorted his elder sisters to the annual Dandaragan Race Meetings, had an eye for the girls. His mother had high hopes of his marriage to a suitable young woman in that district.

'Glendearg'
in ruins, rear view.
Photograph: Robyn Taylor
2003.

After old Ewen Mackintosh's death in 1881 he left 'Glendearg' free of debt, unlike most properties in the district. Euphemia aimed to leave the property in as good a condition for young Ewen to inherit.

Neither of these dreams were fulfilled. At the age of forty-two Ewen married the twenty-five year-old daughter of an Irish labourer who owned a small farm nearby. This did not please Euphemia who became more angry when she learnt how much money he gave to the Catholic priest who performed the ceremony. They were not welcome at 'Glendearg' and chose instead to live on a small farm nearby.

Euphemia in her old age was still very active. One day at the age of 90 while on the verandah entertaining some visitors she noted a snake climbing up. Without a word she sprang to her feet and killed it, and then sat calmly at ease again, to the astonishment of the visitors. She died in 1921, the last survivor of those who arrived on the *Parmelia*.

A year after Euphemia's death her two maiden daughters, Misses Grace and Rose Mackintosh left 'Glendearg' to live in Perth. Ewen and his wife had short tenure of the old homestead. Local gossip said they were unlucky gamblers. In 1923 'Glendearg' was sold to G.T. Gooch, a descendant of John Gooch who died at 'Deepdale' in 1856.

Gooch was a successful pastoralist who planned to establish a sheep stud at 'Glendearg' that could rival that of Hamersley at 'Haseley'. In 1923 he built a fine new mansion at a little distance from the Mackintosh house and named it 'Bacton'. He died suddenly in 1924. The property's former name was restored by the new owner J. C. Phillips of 'Culham'. The next owner was a farmer near Bolgart named Dallas Ludemann, whose son later sold it to Phillips. Some time later it was sold again and by the year 2000 was owned by one of the Hamersley family.

References

Interviews in 1966 with W. Dugdale a Mackintosh descendant, with Thomas Cousins in 1963, Maurice Syred, Mrs Atwell and others.

The plan and sketch of 'Glendearg' were researched and drawn in 1972 by David W.G. Thomas of Darlington and lent by courtesy of E. and V. Ludemann formerly of 'Glendearg'.

31. THE CARROLL

'The Carroll', the name of the northern third of Location 5, is thought to be derived from an Aboriginal word meaning 'rock wallaby'. This land was usually managed in conjunction with 'The Byeen' before J. Butterley bought that property in 1872. A few years later 'The Carroll' was leased by Charles Hennessey who came to the colony in 1862. The annual rental of £15 was paid to a member of the Habgood family. Hennessey occupied a mud bat cottage built possibly in Yule's time as a shepherd's hut. A small spring was used to maintain a kitchen garden. The water was held back by a miniature dam, with sluices to control the flow of water along channels between the garden beds, a method used by most pioneers who maintained a kitchen garden.

'The Carroll'.
Photograph: Robyn Taylor
2002.

'Hennessey's Cottage'
in ruins, built c.1860s.
Photograph: Robyn Taylor
2002.

Nearby was a mulberry tree where Charles Hennessey buried three babies in 1876, 1877 and 1879. His brother Patrick who was living in Scully's old cottage at Bolgart before moving to 'Cowardine' also buried a young daughter there.

Land to the north and east of 'The Carroll' was leased by the Benedictines of New Norcia. An Aboriginal shepherd employed there became very friendly with the Hennesseys. In 1897 he found a small nugget of gold which he showed to Charles. News of the find soon spread and a minor rush of prospectors took place at what was named the Blackboy Hill Goldfield.

The Benedictines were quick to stake a claim, not for gold, but for the freehold of a block of land which was surveyed as a townsite. By the end of the year over 60 claims were pegged by prospectors, and a mining company dug a deep shaft.

Charles Hennessey and a neighbour Mrs Kilpin profited by the sale of meat, milk, butter, eggs and homemade bread. Before the rush petered out Hennessey made enough money to buy land in the Victoria Plains district where he became an independent farmer. 'The Carroll' was bought later by his nephew for £3000. He sold it for £12,000 to W. G. Hawkes of the Koonoona stud in South Australia. The new owner commissioned Charles Osborne, a Perth builder, to erect a substantial brick house. Osborne specialised in stone work and soon found more work at Bolgart replacing old fireplaces with new which were ornamented with distinctive stone mantelpieces.

Joe Pritchard was the manager when 'The Carroll' was bought in 1946 by Ron Travers with financial assistance from the War Veterans Settlement Scheme.

References
Rica Erickson, 'Early Days at Bolgart', in *Early Days,* Journal of Royal W.A. Historical Society, Vol. 6, pt 3, pp. 58-9, 1964.
Interviews with Charles Hennessey's daughter Mrs Adams and Ron Travers.
Henry Martin was the informant regarding the occupancy of Scully's cottage.

32. BEJOORDING

This townsite was declared in 1836 after G. F. Moore and G. Leake explored the Toodyay Valley. It is located at the southern end of Location 5 and was notable for its flowing spring. Bejoording is an Aboriginal word for sleep which indicated to them that it was a safe place for visitors to stay without fear of retribution for trespass. Aborigines gathered there from distant parts for corroborees and to trade, mostly exchanging red ochre handed down from northern regions to be exchanged for white ochre dug from a certain hillside near Bejoording.

Syred's Cottage' at Bejoording, built c.1859. Side view showing additions made in 1870s and 1880s. Photograph: Robyn Taylor 2003.

'Syred's Cottage', built c.1859.

Settlers' stock were watered there but no land was taken up by them until 1856 when notice was given of town lots for sale. Most of the first to purchase land were related by marriage.

The Lots numbered from 1-9 were $3^1/_3$ acres in size, while Lots 10-29 were five acres. Lots 30 and over were as large as 30 acres each, enough for a small farm. John Tomson bought Lots 8-11. Tomson's wife was Sarah Ann Syred whose brothers also bought Bejoording land. Charles Syred had Lots 4 and 27 in August 1858 while William Edward Syred in January 1859 secured Lots 3-7. William's wife was Frances Martin whose brother Alfred Martin bought Lots 12-15 and Number 65 in November 1865.

Prior to these sales Squire Phillips' stock had free access to the Bejoording Spring. When he became aware of the invasion by these men he hastened to buy Lots 5 and 6 in 1859 soon after William Syred made his purchase. By 1875 William bought Lots 3, 20, 22, 24, 28, 29, 30, 55, 57 and 59. In time with Tomson's and Martin's land he had a sizeable farm.

William Syred built a substantial mud bat house and blacksmith shop. He was assured of many customers since there was a lot of traffic along this road and by 1857 old Alex Ferguson who was the favoured blacksmith in the past had died.

The summer months were particularly busy when the roads were dry. Heavy loads of wool and sandalwood were taken by wagon to Guildford from the Victoria Plains and beyond Goomalling and backloaded with stores. William worked at his smithy for most of the year shoeing horses, making the nails and mending wagon wheels and farm machinery.

Charles Syred was a wagoner. He was unmarried and could be away from Bejoording for months at a time. He intended settling down and bought 40 acres of land (Location 454) beside a soak along the Long Hill Road to Goomalling.

The Syreds soon had two neighbours at Bejoording whose wives were sisters and had worked at 'Glendearg' one after the other. John Cousins brought his family to the colony in 1853 and bought Bejoording Lot 34 in 1860. Edward Ralph who arrived in 1860 bought Lot 62 in 1867. They soon became close friends of the Syreds. In 1869 they combined to deepen the well at the Spring, hiring a ticket-of-leave well-sinker named Henry Harding to assist them. After that their wives and children gathered at the well to do the washing on Mondays and made a picnic of it. No doubt the conversation of the mothers included schooling. Mrs Syred tried to teach her children to read by using the labels on flour bags and other items.

Between them by 1870 there were enough children to qualify for a government school. Their application was approved but they had no accommodation for the teacher. Ewen Mackintosh came to their aid by offering rooms for both teacher and school at 'Glendearg'. This school was opened in 1871 and closed in 1874 when the number of scholars declined, and was reopened in 1879 until 1884. The teachers were the Misses Mackintosh.

By then a small community had grown within walking distance of the Syred's home at Bejoording. New land laws were introduced in 1871 known as Special Occupation Leases (SOL). A labourer could become owner of a farm from 100 acres to 500 acres by leasing the land, occupying it and improving it. He was required to pay a deposit of one shilling and sixpence per acre and pay a rental annually for ten years to qualify for a freehold title.

An ambitious and thrifty labourer could become an independent landowner. The former employer welcomed the move since the men usually were available as casual workers during busy seasons without the need to provide them and their families with food and lodgings for the slack periods.

Employees at 'Culham' and 'Glendearg' who became farmers near Bejoording were Beard, Pritchard and Lynch who took up SOL land on the west boundary of the Bejoording Townsite while Lahiff (whose daughter in later years married young Ewen Mackintosh) had SOL 787 and 1257, totalling 150 acres on the eastern boundary.

A new settler in the townsite was Judd Towler who was deaf and dumb and had been wrongly convicted in England. He was given his pardon on arrival in the colony. He made a living as a maker of excellent mud bricks (mud bats) and was nicknamed 'Batty' Towler. His home was built higher up the slope from Syred's home after he married Emily Cousins.

William Syred's son Samuel inherited his Uncle Charles' land along the Long Hill Road and took his wife Elizabeth Ferguson to live there in 1891.

John Cousins' sons William and George each bought 400-acre farm blocks along the same road to Goomalling. William named his Location 1311 as 'Long Hill Farm' while George named his as 'Orleans Farm'. Both built simple mud brick cottages with the help of Batty Towler, and when their families grew larger, they added more rooms.

Another new settler at Bejoording was John Lucas who migrated from England in 1886 when railways were being built in the colony. Proposals were made in the 1890s to extend the railway from Toodyay to Bolgart. Bejoording was expected to become a thriving town. Lucas bought eighty acres there, but when the Goldfields railway was extended from Northam instead of Toodyay, these expectations faded. Mrs Lucas made a small income by manning the Bejoording telephone exchange.

By then the Bejoording community was large enough to warrant visits by an Anglican clergyman from Toodyay who at first conducted services in the limited space of the original Syred home. He became concerned about the number of illiterate children in the district and persuaded the parents to build a mud brick school under the guidance of Batty Towler. Used primarily as a school and a place in which to conduct services on Sundays, it soon became a popular, if small, community centre. It remained in use until 1912, after which it was demolished and the building material was salvaged for use elsewhere.

There was no land available for farming on the modern scale, which required at least 1000 acres and preferably 2000 acres. The old pastoral leases in the vicinity of Bolgart were resumed by the Government for subdivision and sold by auction in 1903 and 1908. The railway from Toodyay to Bolgart which was opened in 1909 saw the rise of a larger community at Bolgart and the decline of Bejoording.

The third generation of original Bejoording settlers were assuming management of their fathers' farms. William Cousins' son Herbert built a new home at 'Long Hill Farm'. Although mud bricks were used, the doors and windows were framed with burnt bricks. His bungalow home was sheltered by verandahs and the roof was of galvanised iron.

At 'Orleans Farm', George Cousins' son Thomas was content to add a wing to his parents' house. He faced the mud brick walls with stone and added a wing and a verandah.

'Orleans Farm' built c.1900 for
G. T. Cousins.
Photograph 1997.
Courtesy of Leo Camerer.

Syred's house and Ralph's Cottage at Bejoording remained almost unchanged except for iron roofing which replaced the thatch. When the Bejoording school was closed the children then attended Wattening school. The building of a hotel and an Agricultural Hall at Bolgart, as well as tennis courts and a football field drained the activities away from Bejoording to that centre. But Bejoording did not die. By the end of the 1980s a new group of people came to live at the old townsite. They were curious to learn its history. Peter Syred still occupied the land taken up by his ancestor but had built a modern house a little further up the slope. The old original house was still in excellent condition. It was given heritage status and entrusted to the Toodyay Shire Council. It is a worthy monument to those who first lived at Bejoording.

References
The Toodyay Herald.
Interviews with descendants of Syred, Ralph, Beard, Lucas and Tyndall.

33. WATTENING

'Wattening' developed as a community in the early 1900s. Squire Phillips' pastoral leases of the 1850s were acquired by Bishop Salvado in the 1870s and were granted as freehold to the Midland Railway Company in the 1890s. When the goldfields were booming there were demands for opening up huge areas for farming. The Government resumed the pastoral leases around the Wattening and Bolgart Springs and auctions were held in 1903 and 1908 of blocks usually about 1000 acres, although by then the traditional single-furrow plough was replaced by modern machinery. Most farmers required up to 2000 acres and bought more than one block.

Plaque commemorating the site of Wattening School. Photograph Robyn Taylor 2003.

Among the first purchasers of land at Wattening were descendants of the Bejoording families, including Syreds, Cousins and Cook. Those from the Eastern States included Camerer, Ludemann, Jacob and the Hanson brothers. Their nearest social centre was Bejoording and the nearest public hall was the Culham Agricultural Hall. The nearest railway was at Toodyay.

The children of Wattening walked or rode or were driven to the Bejoording school. Their parents attended Culham Hall for sports, dances and public meetings, such as those held to discuss the need for a railway at least as far as the Bolgart Water Reserve.

The people at Wattening supported Maxmillian Camerer when he proposed the building of a hall near his home to be used as a school and where divine service and social events could be held. The Temperance Hall was opened in 1912 where a dance was held and attendants at a sports day contributed to the cost. The Wattening School was opened that year. The Bejoording School was then closed, and its pupils as well as some from Bolgart attended the new Wattening School.

There was a strong sense of community at Wattening where a very active Tennis Club was formed using a clay court put down by the Ludemann family at their home 'Fernlea'. After the creation of new tennis courts of asphalt at Bolgart the Wattening members joined that Club. The building of St Augustine's Anglican Church at Bolgart in 1939 was fully supported by the Wattening settlers. After a school bus took the Wattening children to the Toodyay School in 1947 the Wattening Hall served no purpose and was demolished. The only sign of its existence as the social centre for the small community at Wattening is a plaque by the roadside.

References

Camerer family papers, with permission of Leo Camerer.
Ludemann notes, courtesy of the Ludemann family.
Frank Jacob. *The Winding Track. The History of Stephen Hall Jacob Family, 1815-1996*, Privately published.

34. HALCYON

'Halcyon' is the Wattening farm developed by Maxmillian Rudolph Camerer (1834-1913) who came from Victoria in 1903 in search of good farm land. He had migrated from Germany in the 1860s and settled in the Wimmera district where he became a prominent dairy farmer, building a butter factory to his own plans. The Victorian bank failures in the 1890s caused him to sell his property and to open a retail business in Melbourne in partnership with his sons. They lived comfortably in a two-storeyed house with stables and coachhouse attached.

'Halcyon', formerly 'Lichtenthal'. Photograph: Robyn Taylor 2002.

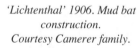

'Lichtenthal' 1906. Mud bat construction. Courtesy Camerer family.

However the sons hankered for a rural life. Land in Western Australian was comparatively cheap. They bought Lots 14, 15 and 17 at Wattening and wound up the Melbourne business. In 1904 the whole family sailed to Fremantle prepared to be pioneers on uncleared land.

They left Fremantle in three covered wagons loaded with stores, camping gear and implements as well as pigs, whose squealing created quite a stir as they passed through Toodyay. They became bogged at Wattening Brook so they set up tents for the men and a galvanised hut was built for Mrs Camerer and the daughters. These they occupied for two years.

In that time land was cleared, a dairy herd was established and mud bricks were made for a large house. The walls were waterproofed by painting them with boiling linseed oil. Their home was originally named 'Lichtenthal' meaning 'Light in the Valley', possibly because their lights at night could be seen across the valley by their friend Captain Hanson. Hanson's small Wattening land (Lot 16) had been chosen for him by the Camerers. Although he was accustomed to tall masts swaying he was most apprehensive of the tall trees he was clearing when they swayed in the breeze. At night he was even more afraid and welcomed the sight of the lights at 'Lichtenthal'.

At first the Camerers depended on the sale of their butter at Northam for an income. This was taken in wet bags slung from the roof of a covered wagon to keep it cool. In 1906 the Camerers with Captain Hanson and his brother and a neighbour, Edward Ludemann, attended a large public meeting at the Culham Agricultural Hall. A motion was passed asking for the railway at Toodyay to be extended up the Valley to serve the needs of the farmers, at least as far as Bejoording. Shortly after this Hanson's brother suffered an accident. They sold their land to Camerer and left the district.

The Camerer's commodious home 'Lichtenthal' became a centre for friends to visit on Sundays to attend a service conducted by Maxmillian who was a lay preacher. They sang hymns around the organ played by the women of the family. Maxmillian died in 1913 and his son Rudolph followed his example.

During World War I the family was scarcely affected by anti-German sentiment. When the war ended Rudolph built additions to his home. He made and fired his bricks and then employed a man from Perth named Cook to build a large living room and an imposing turret. These were connected to the original home by a breezeway. He renamed his house 'Halcyon' meaning peace. An orange grove at the front created a pleasing view from the road. A driveway to the back of the house was excavated from the hillside.

The Camerer family was unaware of the Aboriginal story about this hill told to G. F. Moore in 1836 that it was the home of a Chingah, an awesome spirit with a big head and horns, much feared by Aborigines. It could have been one of the cattle escaped from the Swan district in the 1830s. The Camerer's dairy herd grazed near the same spot.

References
Camerer papers and interviews with the family.

35. FERNLEA

'Fernlea' on lots 804, 10 and 13 at Wattening were bought by Edward Ludemann of Victoria about 1906. In 1901 he had come to Western Australia to work in the Goldfields as an engine driver on the Great Boulder Mine, but decided to go farming. His partner Wheelwright was his brother-in-law, who with a mate named Gray, owned 595 acres. A sister in Bendigo also bought a block which Ludemann farmed on her behalf. The subsequent amalgamation of these blocks made farming at 'Fernlea' possible on a larger scale.

'Fernlea'.
Photograph: Robyn Taylor 2003.

The Ludemann's first home at Wattening was a typical Goldfields camp of the better type. It was two-roomed, and timber-framed with walls of flat iron and a galvanised iron roof. A bough shed on one side served as a kitchen. When a new house was built, bricks were made and fired on the spot by Henry Davey, son of the Toodyay builder.

The original galvanised iron camp became the kitchen. It was moved to the new site on rollers cut from a wandoo tree, adopting a method often seen on the goldfields when a house was moved on jinkers with huge wheels. This iron-walled kitchen was very hot in summer and was replaced later by a large kitchen-family room of brick.

The Ludemann and Camerer families shared a German origin and became more closely linked in 1918 when Alice Ludemann married Rudolph Camerer. Both were tennis enthusiasts and on weekends joined in the competition on the tennis court at 'Fernlea'. It was made of white-ant mounds crushed and puddled to make a very hard surface. A tennis club was formed in 1920 which functioned until 1930, the time when the Bolgart Tennis Club covered their ant-heap courts with a harder surface.

In 1924 about the time that Edward Ludemann became Chairman of the Toodyay Roads Board he bought a Ford car. He also enlarged his farm by the purchase of 1196 acres. His son Dallas occupied 690 acres, the part of 'Glendearg' that included Benbengaddading hill on which Surveyor Smythe had placed a survey peg in 1837. Dallas used a tractor to clear his land and sold the logs and went further afield to cut sandalwood. In 1927 he married Valerie Wright, a descendant of J. P. Smith of 'Baylie Farm'. He built a fine Federation style home of fired brick and reared a family there. When he required a larger area of farmland he bought 5000 acres along the Bolgart-Goomalling Road and later extended his interests by the purchase of 'Glendearg' where his son Ted lived. The Bolgart-Goomalling block of 5000 acres was sold in 1953 and 'Glendearg' was relinquished later.

'Fernlea' which was inherited by Harry Ludemann remained in family hands. The Ludemann's services in local Government were to extend over three generations. Edward Ludemann was a member of the Toodyay Shire Council for twenty-two years, his son Dallas for twenty-three years and his grandson Geoffrey for twenty-eight years.

References
Family notes and interviews

36. HILL 60

'Hill 60' on Lot 803 at Wattening was given this name by Charles Syred, a veteran of World War I. The steep conical hill beside the house reminded him of a similar hill in Belgium where British and Australian soldiers battled desperately to keep it from German hands. After he returned from the War he bought the farm from Henry Jacob and named it

'Bedowan', (Hill 60).
Photograph: Beth Field.

after that Belgian hill. The Aboriginal name of Bedswan, indicated on early maps, was then forgotten.

Jacob was an Englishman who migrated to Victoria in 1887 and then worked in South Australia before joining the gold rush into Western Australia. He arrived at Fremantle in 1894 and went to work in the country. By 1909 he was at Bakers Hill where he became acquainted with the Smith family, also from South Australia.

Henry Jacob married Elizabeth Smith and bought land at Wattening. A mud brick cottage was their home and by 1912 it had been enlarged by adding rooms of fired brick. The original walls were faced with stone. By the year 2000 when the inner walls were exposed by cracks in the plaster the mud bricks were exposed. Henry Jacob with his wife and five children sold this farm in 1923 to go farming on a larger scale in the Bruce Rock district where the Smith family was settled.

The new owner Charles Syred and his wife Rene had two sons. The boys used to play around the slopes of the steep little hill and attempted to climb it occasionally in games like King of the Castle. They would have been interested to hear the story of the Aboriginal who stood on the summit defying avengers.

References
Frank Jacob, *The Winding Track, The History of Stephen Hall Jacob Family 1815-1996*. Privately published.

G.F. Moore, *Diary of Ten Years' Eventful Life of an Early Settler in Western Australia*, London Edition, 1884. Facsimile edition UWA Press, Nedlands 1978.

Interviews with members of the Syred family.

37. SCULLY'S FARM AND BOLGART, OLD AND NEW

'Scully's Farm' and Bolgart were adjacent to the Bolgart Water Reserve which was set aside in 1836 for the use of travellers and stock. Aborigines spoke of Bolgart as the winter haunt of the magic snake which in the summer months made its way down the Toodyay Valley and up the Avon to the deep Burlong Pool near Northam.

Survey peg for townsite at Blackboy Hill gold diggings, 1897. Now a Bolgart farm.

Bolgart people celebrated the year 2000 by erecting their own Bell Tower beside their Hall.

The first white settler at Bolgart was Captain Scully of the 80th Foot Regiment who arrived in the colony in 1839. He leased Yule's 15,000 acre grant known as 'The Byeen' and was to receive the northern third (known as 'Bullegine') in return for performing the location duties. As there was little water on this section Scully bought a homestead block of seventy acres along one boundary of the Bolgart Water Reserve which was only a short distance from Yule's boundary. He built his homestead there and cultivated a kitchen garden and grew enough wheat to maintain his employees in flour for a year.

Bolgart was the northernmost farm in the colony. Scully became Resident Magistrate of the Toodyay district which by then extended from Northam north to the pastoral leases of the Victoria Plains. Settlers who came to him on official business found this isolation to be most inconvenient and some preferred to stay overnight.

Scully had a comfortable cottage of several rooms. His devoted Irish housekeeper lived in a separate cottage where the kitchen and storeroom were located. His labourers slept in a slab hut or the barn. Two Scottish shepherds, John and Donald Macpherson lived in outstation huts at 'The Byeen' and a short distance up the Bolgart Brook.

By 1841 settlers in the Toodyay Valley needed more land for their wide-ranging stock. Scully with James Drummond, the botanist, and Samuel P. Phillips explored north of Bolgart as far as the Moore River. Within a few years several shepherds were minding flocks of sheep in that remote region.

Scully is remembered chiefly for the assistance he gave to a small band of Benedictine missionaries who came to evangelise the Aborigines at a place on the Moore River which they named New Norcia. When Scully returned to Ireland early in 1847 he leased Bolgart to the Lefroy brothers.

Gerald De Courcy Lefroy had scarcely moved into Scully's cottage when the servants' quarters were burnt to the ground and the married couple lost all their belongings. While it was being rebuilt Gerald gave up his bedroom to the wife while he and the husband slept in the barn. It took several weeks to rebuild the servants' quarters which Gerald replaced exactly as before. It was forty-three feet by fourteen feet with slab timber walls, plastered inside with mud. The chimney was of stone and the roof thatched with blackboy tops.

Since the best pastoral land along the Moore River was already taken up by others, Gerald explored further north and leased land at 'Bebano'. This he soon extended and gave it the name of 'Walebing'.

To maintain the two establishments of Bolgart and Walebing Gerald required more staff. Some Parkhurst boys were expected on the *Orient* in October 1848 and Lefroy went to Fremantle to select some. Among the free passengers were Edward Butler Beere and his wife and family. He was of the genteel class in Dublin and Lefroy felt sorry for them. He offered the tenancy of Bolgart while he was moving to Walebing, furniture included. Lefroy was soon disillusioned about the family's ability to manage the cottage properly. Beere badgered his wife and was bad tempered with the daughters. None of them seemed capable of fending for themselves and his precious dining room table suffered when Mrs Beere used it as a cutting board.

In 1842 Lefroy took his bride to his newly built substantial house at 'Walebing', one of the first homesteads to have a galvanized iron roof. Then the partnership with his brother was severed and he sailed with his wife to India with a cargo of horses owned by his father-in-law before proceeding to Ireland.

Gerald de Courcy Lefroy's shepherds Dollard and Higgins owned small flocks of their own by then. They brought them to the Bolgart Water Reserve and bought ten acres along one of the boundaries. It is thought that they built the cottage that was located a short distance up the Bolgart Brook near where seventy years later the Bolgart Hotel was built. They sold it in the 1860s and it was occupied by another of the shepherds from the Victoria Plains, Isaac Doust, and after that his daughter and her husband Henry Green lived in that cottage for many years.

Higgins block was soon sold to Squire Phillips whose horses had free range. In summer months when distant water holes dried up the horses came to drink at the Bolgart Bog so special stockyards were built there to trap the horses for branding. Phillips employed Charles Chitty to manage the Bolgart runs. He lived there until 1881 when he leased 'Batbatting' in the Goomalling district. The Bolgart cottage was then occupied for a year or so by Patrick Hennessey.

Bolgart's modern history as a town could have began in 1898 after the Benedictines surveyed a townsite at the Blackboy Hill diggings. This area of pastoral country was sold as farm blocks in 1903 after which the new settlers asked the Government to build a railway from Toodyay. The steam engines required water so the terminus was at the Bolgart Water Reserve where a townsite was surveyed in 1909.

Apart from the stationmaster the inhabitants included a butcher, a baker and a bootmaker as well as three blacksmiths and two boarding house keepers, one of whom opened a store and post office. Railway workers, who were extending the railway further north, camped in tents beside the Brook. An Agricultural Hall was built in 1913 which served as a school. Ant heap tennis courts further up the slope were fenced to keep out foraging fowls belonging to the mother of one of the blacksmiths, who had the foresight to build on higher ground.

Within a few years the Bolgart Bog began to spread and the railway yards became a quagmire. In 1914 a new townsite was gazetted higher up the hill slope. The people near the Reserve were reluctant to move until a high flood in 1915 damaged some buildings and washed away the railway workers' camps. Another incentive to move was the building of a State Hotel at the new site. The tennis courts near the Bog survived and the original Bolgart Hall continued to function as a schoolroom until January 1932 when it was burnt down. After that catastrophe the children were taught for two years in a beekeeper's mud bat hut located at the new townsite. By 1934 a vacant country school, already twice moved, was transported in three sections to Bolgart. The flooring was better than the dirt floor of the beekeeper's hut despite the ominous creaking at the joins. When a school bus service was introduced in 1949 the number of pupils increased and two teachers were required. A vacant store in the town then became the school until 1951 when a cement brick school was built.

This tardy response by the Government to children's needs was in sharp contrast to the speedy reaction of the community to build another hall when the old Bolgart Agricultural Hall was burnt down in 1932. Without aid from either the Government or the Roads Board a local committee raised funds for the building of a new hall located in the second townsite. When it required improvements in 1952 the committee bought the vacant Culham Hall, demolished it and used the bricks to add a porch and other amenities to their own. The tennis courts, which had been relocated beside the Hall, were then surfaced with bitumen (known as Colas). The nine-hole golf course which had been laid out through vacant town lots and along the railway line was replaced by an eighteen-hole course. In 1953 nearly ninety acres were bought from Charles Syred. The football field beside the Hall had a slope varying from seventeen feet to four feet. This was levelled in 1955 by volunteers, working with machinery lent by both the Victoria Plains and Toodyay Roads Boards and also Plaimars Ltd of Toodyay. Electricity was introduced in 1962 and water piped to the town shortly after.

These amenities encouraged local farmers to retire to Bolgart town. It progressed while other small country towns declined. By community effort a bell tower was built in 1999. The original idea rose from a 'tongue-in-cheek' suggestion that it might result in as much publicity as the Perth Bell Tower. The resulting publicity drew busloads of sightseers and promoted the town's attractions.

Scully's cottage had long since disappeared. In 1960 the old cottage was recognised only by a patch of red earth in a field of clover and capeweed. When this was shown to a Benedictine priest that year he knelt down and kissed the ground, paying homage to Captain Scully, the benefactor of the missionaries who founded New Norcia. The site is now covered by a dense growth of shrubs and trees, nurtured by the ever-spreading waters of the Bolgart Bog.

The Agricultural Hall at the original townsite was used as a schoolroom. Pupils playing jump the rope, 1930. Courtesy Jean Lovelock.

Open air lessons. Pupils left to right: Karl Long, Bobbie Kilpatrick, Marjorie Smith, Joan Travers, Roma Kilpatrick, ...(?), Betty Kilpatrick, Mollie Owens, with Dick Rice and Ron Travers in the background. Courtesy Jean Lovelock.

After the old hall was burnt down the children were taught in the beekeeper's Honey House at the new townsite. The State Hotel is on the right. Courtesy Jean Lovelock.

The first one-teacher Government School, 1934. Pupils preparing a garden. Teacher R. Erickson. Courtesy Jean Lovelock.

Pupil numbers increased. Cook and Smith's vacant store was used as a two-teacher school at Bolgart.

Bolgart School. Photograph: Robyn Taylor 2003.

References

Rica Erickson, 'Early Days at Bolgart', in *Early Days*, Journal of the Royal Western Historical Society. Vol. 6, pt 3, 1964, pp.46-61.

Interviews with descendants of Chitty, Doust, Green, Podd, Syred, Smith and Edna Falconer, daughter of W. Smith one of the storekeepers at the Bog.

38. WYENING MISSION

Wyening Mission is located on 12 acres of land (Location 233) which was owned originally by S. P. Phillips and A. Lee Steere. A permanent spring at the site was the centre for their huge pastoral leases north of Bolgart.

In December 1878 these pastoral leases were taken over by Bishop Salvado who added 400 acres of freehold land. A farm was established, capable in time of supporting the needs of fifteen or more shepherds employed at the outstations. In 1880 a track was cleared from New Norcia to 'Wyening', and a simple hut was built where some monks were stationed. Their chief duty was to distribute the rations to the shepherds who were mostly Aborigines.

Wells were sunk at the Mission and also at the outcamps. At least two expirees named Hoffman and Ross were employed as well sinkers but much of the work was done by the monks.

The method of building these mission wells was to locate the site by water divining and then to dig down for fifteen to thirty feet until the pick struck the vein of water. A stone wall about eighteen inches thick and twelve feet across was then built around the waterhole. The Mission built about fifty-eight wells similar to this on its many pastoral leases.

In time the simple bush hut at Wyening Mission was replaced by a substantial building. John Powell and John Smith, both expirees, contracted to produce 50,200 bricks. Two Benedictine stonemasons, Brothers Basileo and Adeodata, completed the building in 1892. When Edward Chitty was engaged as the farm manager yet another substantial house was built to accommodate him and his family. By 1906 he was cropping about 100 acres of wheat and had planted five acres of vines from parent stock introduced at New Norcia about thirty years before.

When the old pastoral leases around Wyening were cancelled to be subdivided as farms, Chitty's home at the Mission became a popular meeting place for the newcomers. There they discussed such matters as the need for a regular delivery of mails and also for an extension of the railway from Bolgart.

For some years religious services had been held at the Wyening Mission to meet the spiritual needs of the Benedictine brothers and the two families in the locality who regularly attended this monthly celebration of Mass. After the sale of the pastoral land several newcomers

'Wyening Mission'
Photograph: Beth Field
2003.

The Winery at 'Wyening
Mission'.
Photograph: Beth Field
2003.

Winery Cellars.
Photograph: Beth Field
2003.

The Well at 'Wyening
Mission'.
Photograph: Beth Field
2003.

to the district joined this congregation. Before long Sunday picnics at the Wyening Spring were a regular occurrence. Cricket was played, a football was kicked, and some of the men bought wine made by the Benedictines at New Norcia from grapes grown by Chitty at the Wyening Mission.

At first the grapes were harvested by the Aborigines, but later they were picked by boys from St Ildephonsus College who regarded the event as a holiday, enriched by the freedom given to eat as many grapes as they wished. The grapes were crushed at the Mission and the juice taken to New Norcia for fermenting and processing. About 15,000 gallons (67,000 litres) were produced annually. Plans were made for the whole operation to take place at the Wyening Mission. Stone was quarried from the hillside and the winery was built during World War I by Charles Bianchini-Marsella and others.

The walls of the winery were 40 feet high and two feet thick, sturdy enough to last a thousand years. It was built on two levels butting into the hillslope. Grapes were brought to the top-level where they were tipped into large containers which could be moved on rails after they were filled. After the crushing the juice was drained to the lower level for processing and finally poured into rows of casks on ground level. Power was provided by a small engine driven by steam.

During the economic depression which followed World War I Chitty's services as manager of the Wyening Farm were terminated and the vineyards were neglected. The Mission House was occupied by some Spanish-speaking lay brothers and Father Felix who was appointed as parish priest from 1923 to 1949. He preached in broken English in a wooden Church of St Joseph at Bolgart. His successor Father Michael from the Eastern States was instrumental in replacing this little church with a fine brick and tile building in 1960.

One of Father Michael's first duties was to restore the Mission as a farm. In 1949 an immigrant from Yugoslavia named Gustl Schwarzbach was engaged as a farm manager and winemaker at 'Wyening'. The manager's house was renovated to accommodate his family. They arrived by train on a hot summer's day clad in their best serge suits to be driven in a cart to the Mission. Gustl, an experienced winemaker, energetically extended the vineyard to cover forty-five acres. His wife Ellie grew a fine vegetable garden. She was given permission to convert one of the Mission rooms to serve as a small chapel when Father Michael once more held religious services at the Mission.

By 1970 Gustl Schwarzbach produced the best vintage ever, but in 1972 the Abbot decided to concentrate the Benedictine land holdings at New Norcia. A Wyening farmer named John Young owned land near New Norcia. It suited them both to exchange.

The Schwarzbach family connection with the Wyening Mission was deeply rooted. They were invited to stay there when John Young owned the place but Gustl was growing old. After a year or so he and Ellie decided to retire to a milder climate at Bridgetown.

The vineyards at Wyening Mission once more became neglected. The wine-making machinery was transferred to New Norcia, leaving some of the casks and a few fittings for John Young who hoped to create a wine-making museum there.

Anxious to preserve the historic winery rather than use it as a barn the Young family recruited committee members to assist in its restoration and preservation. The place was opened by appointment for tours of inspection. Forty people at a time could be catered for at luncheons and other suitable functions. The Mission was then listed as having heritage value.

References

Interviews with members of the families of Chitty, Harrington and Schwarzbach.

Wyening Mission and Winery, Victoria Plains. Conservation Plan, Considine & Griffiths, Architects Pty. Ltd., with Dorothy Erickson, December 1996.

Dom Williams, 'A Survey of the Correspondence between Bishop Salvado and John Forrest' in *Early Days*, Volume 5, Journal of the Royal Western Australian Historical Society.

'Wyening Mission Farm' logo.
Photograph: Beth Field 2003.

39. NEW NORCIA

The Benedictine Mission at New Norcia was founded by a party of Catholic evangelists, mostly Spanish, who arrived under the leadership of Bishop Brady in 1846. Their purpose was to evangelise the Aborigines. They were guided to the site on the Moore River by Captain Scully's wagoners. A Government grant of twenty acres of land was augmented by the purchase of 2560 acres, which became the site of the monastery, the only one of its kind in Australia.

During 1848 Bishop Brady sent Dom Serra to Europe to seek funds and recruitments. He was soon followed to Rome by Dom Salvado on the same mission. Both men were consecrated as Bishops before returning to Western Australia. Serra was appointed as administrator of the diocese of Perth which led to acrimonious quarrels with Brady who then departed. Bishop Salvado's diocese was to be in the Northern Territory, but before he could take up duties, that settlement was abandoned. So he remained in Western Australia and later was given the diocese of New Norcia.

Under Salvado's guidance the Mission at New Norcia made outstanding progress, supported largely by an income from an increasing pastoral empire. The leaseholds by the 1880s extended over almost a million acres. They were located around small freehold blocks of land where waterholes and springs were converted to permanent supplies by the building of large stone wells. Ticket-of-leave men and expirees were employed on this work as well as some of the lay brothers. Mission farms were established at 'Marah' to the north near Watheroo and also at Wyening near Bolgart to the south.

A small village grew around the Mission at New Norcia. It was almost self-supporting with vegetable gardens, wheat fields and flourmill, vineyards, an olive grove, an apiary. Building proceeded at a rate faster than the Benedictines could manage alone. At first helpers came from Perth. At least one expiree Charles Johnson, was engaged as a carpenter.

Schools were built for Aboriginal children as well as houses for their parents. A post office was opened in 1867. When the telegraph line was constructed to connect Perth with Geraldton it passed through New Norcia where an Aboriginal woman was trained as the telegraphist. A police station was opened, and another school was built for the children of the colonists who were settling at or near New Norcia. In the late

1. Post Office
2. St. Joseph's Convent and School for Girls
3. Monastery
4. Hotel
5. Pro-Cathedral
6. St. Gertrude's Girls' College
7. Olive Press and Power-house
8. Police Station
9. College Classrooms
10. Machinery Sheds
11. St. Benedict's Boys' College
12. Old Blacksmith's Shop
13. St. Mary's House for Boys
14. New Flour Mill
15. Old Flour Mill

Aerial view of New Norcia, c.1980. Benedictine Community of New Norcia Photographic collection.

A distinguished lady visitor is welcomed at the Mission gates, c.1880.
Benedictine Community of New Norcia Photographic collection, 74348P.

1880s a doctor's residence was built to house a medical officer, the first of whom was a son of Daniel Connor of Toodyay. The Victoria Plains Roads Board meetings were held at New Norcia during 1887-1904. Rainfall records required by the State Meteorological Department were kept regularly from 1882 onwards.

New Norcia had all the facilities of a country town, but when plans were made for a railway to be built to connect Perth with Geraldton Bishop Salvado strongly opposed the proposal for it to follow the road through Mission land. He feared this exposure to civilisation would undermine the Mission's work with Aborigines. His appointment in 1887 as a Protector of Natives gave weight to his objections. Also like his neighbouring pastoralists he feared the loss of many thousands of acres of valuable pastoral leases. He pointed out the fact that a route through Mogumber to the west would be 70 miles shorter and this was a deciding factor in his favour.

Bishop Salvado made several visits to Europe and usually returned with precious gifts of books, paintings and vestments. At the same time he was negotiating with the Western Australian Government to secure benefits bestowed upon charitable institutions. These were granted in 1898 in the year of his Jubilee as a bishop. He returned to Rome that year planning to overview the selection of his successor, but died there in 1900.

In 1901 Abbot Torres was appointed to take charge at New Norcia and was responsible for bringing Salvado's remains for internment in the Chapel. Under Torres' guidance Salvado's plans of evangelising Aborigines switched from New Norcia to the establishment of a mission at Kalumburu in the far north of the State. The Aboriginal schools at New Norcia were enlarged and improved and plans were made for New Norcia to be a centre of learning for white children who needed a higher education. St Gertrude's College for Girls was opened in 1903 while St Ildephonsus' College for Boys was opened ten years later. The monastery building were enlarged and beautified. Abbot Torres was consecrated as Bishop in 1910, and died in 1913.

Abbot Catalan succeeded Torres and was responsible for the building of an imposing hotel or guesthouse, judged to be adequate for accommodation by a papal delegation. It was used instead by parents of College students.

The Great War of 1914-18 and the severe economic recession which

St Mary's Church.
Photograph:
Beth Field, 2003.

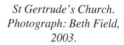

St Gertrude's Church.
Photograph: Beth Field,
2003.

followed retarded further progress at New Norcia. Fewer Spaniards came to join the community and fewer children were enrolled at the Colleges when the Government opened more secondary high schools in country districts.

145

By the time of World War II maintenance of the historic buildings at New Norcia was burdensome. To win some revenue to prevent their decay the less conservative Australian recruits to the Benedictine order introduced the radical idea of a museum and art gallery for the exhibition of their priceless treasures. This inspired the formation of a generous body of laymen known as The Friends of New Norcia, dedicated to the restoration of New Norcia's buildings. Festivals and seminars were organised and grants of money were obtained. Motel accommodation was offered in one of the Mission buildings.

The changes from evangelical and educational aims was not taken lightly, but they brought new life to the historic institution. There is no loss of dignity or serenity while the Benedictine order continues its customary observance of religious rites.

References

The Story of New Norcia by the Benedictine Order of New Norica, (undated). Battye Stack 266 STO.

P. McCarthy, 'Catholicism in WA 1829-1911', in *University Studies,* 2/994.

Royal Commission, 1905.

Notes from Dom William, Father Michael, Father Bernard and Abbot Placid Spearritt.

40. GLENTROMIE

'Glentromie' has the distinction of being part of the first pastoral lease registered in the colony of Western Australia. In 1841 Captain Scully and his party explored the region and named the Victoria Plains and the Moore River. About a year later Scully sent his shepherds Donald and John Macpherson there in charge of his sheep.

The Macphersons would have heard of a Shepherds Club proposed at a meeting at York in January 1843. The aim was to protect members from unfair dismissal before their indentures expired. Incompetent shepherds lost their jobs but a good shepherd expected to continue employment even when the price of wool began to decline in 1842. Some employers were offering sheep in lieu of wages, a proposal that would have been welcomed by the Macpherson brothers. Their sheep could be shepherded with Scully's until the flock grew too large. A sober and thrifty shepherd could own as many sheep as his master's original flock within seven years.

'Glentromie', 1960s.
Courtesy of Nixon family.

Shepherds knew where the best grazing was to be found on those distant runs far beyond settlement. When they had enough sheep of their own there was competition for grazing in those parts.

The Governor objected to the free use of Crown Land and in 1845 introduced a system of pastoral leases. A shepherd who had some sheep of his own could at small cost secure legal right to large areas of land, with the first right to purchase a small acreage around the waterhole. Competition for pastoral land was then lessened.

This was the situation when Donald Macpherson leased 10,000 acres, including Badji Badji, Noondagoonda, and Murra Murra, which was the area he later named as 'Glentromie'. His small flock of sheep was

147

augmented by the addition of those of his brother John, his cousin Ewen Mackintosh, and a fellow Scot named John Davidson. They enlarged the lease in 1847 and 1848 to 20,000 acres, registered in the name of the Scotch Shepherds by Ewen Mackintosh.

By 1850 their combined flocks were large enough for each to select his own pastoral lease. Mackintosh and Davidson leased land further down the Moore River while Donald Macpherson retained the original lease, naming it 'Glentromie'. In 1853 he married Jessie McKnoe. They lived in a mud hut and shared all the difficulties of a pioneering life. By 1855 Donald owned 4000 sheep and held 100,000 acres of pastoral leasehold. He cropped 100 acres of wheat to maintain his staff's needs in flour. By 1860 he held 30 small freehold blocks of land at various waterholes and by 1870 had doubled that number and increased his pastoral leases.

In 1869 he began building a grand new home to accommodate their large family of eight children. The new 'Glentromie' was built of kiln-fired bricks. Among the ticket-of-leave employees were a bricklayer named William Butler, and three carpenters, Patrick Byrne, Dan Stevenson and James Taylor. Jessie was pregnant and looked forward to the comfort of the new house. But the child died young and Jessie did not live to see the completion of the building.

After Jessie's death in August 1869 her eldest daughter Jessie, at fourteen years of age, was left in charge of the household as well as three young sisters and four brothers, the eldest being fifteen years old.

Donald Macpherson then employed Selena Earnshaw, a schoolteacher, as housekeeper and governess. They were married in January 1871. He was elected that year to the newly created Victoria Plains Road Board and was its chairman.

The meetings were held at 'Glentromie' until H.B. Lefroy was elected as chairman in 1876. Donald Macpherson remained as a member of the Board until 1886. Selena was a busy hostess. In 1879 the second race meeting in the Victoria Plains was held at 'Glentromie', to be followed by a grand ball.

A major source of Donald's income was the sale of horses to India. When this trade declined his horses were sent to Java. In 1874 his eldest son Aneas at twenty years of age was in charge of a shipment of horses sent to Batavia. Younger sons made the same journey in turn, as one after the other the brothers went to the Northwest to manage their own pastoral stations.

A fire in 1881 destroyed the flour mill and damaged other buildings at 'Glentromie'. They were not insured but Macpherson began the expensive task of replacing them. Also the stables and outbuildings needed enlarging. He employed two Chinese named Ah Hee and Al Koon as bricklayers who had just finished working at 'Berkshire Valley'. They were housed at the Aborigines' camp and complained when they saw the other employees were housed in cottages, two for married men and one of two rooms for single men. When their complaints were not heard they absconded before the work was finished and sought redress from the Resident Magistrate at Toodyay. Since no contracts had been signed their tools and belongings were restored to them.

Early in 1887 Donald Macpherson although recently recovered from illness, entertained nine visitors from Perth. He showed them around

'Glentromie' and its complex of buildings. Apart from the homestead with its eleven rooms and large kitchen and storeroom there was a seven-room cottage with a cellar capable of storing 2000 gallons of wine produced from his vines. Three other cottages accommodated the rest of his employees. His mill was rebuilt and nearby were stables built of fired brick, 100 feet long and with walls twenty feet high to include a loft holding fifty tons of hay. The horses were stabled in twenty-seven stalls and four loose boxes. Alongside was a cart shed, with harness room and chaff house as well as a blacksmithy. The shearing shed housed a wool press. Half of the 250 acres cleared for farming was sown with wheat annually. Macpherson depended upon a dung heap for fertilizer.

Macpherson owned 6000 acres of freehold which he was fencing with wire, 30 miles of it being sheep-proof and twelve miles to enclose paddocks for horses and cattle. However most of his 8000 sheep were still shepherded over his leases, totalling 150,000 acres. His stock included 250 horses, 150 cattle and 100 pigs. This was a property to be proud of.

Donald was aware that his eldest daughter had more than a passing fancy for an employee named Andrew Smith. He strongly disapproved when they proposed marriage. Family tradition has it that they eloped. Whether this occurred before his death in 1887 is not known. They were married in February 1888 and their two sons Keith and Ross were born in Adelaide in 1890 and 1892. They became famous aviators and both were knighted for their achievements.

At the time of Donald Macpherson's death in August 1887 he was deeply in debt. The major creditors were the merchants Padbury and Loton. They bought 'Glentromie' for £11,200. C.K. Davidson, who had married Padbury's niece, was installed as manager. Padbury had no children and 'Glentromie' was inherited by Davidson and his wife.

Davidson became a prominent member of the Victoria Plains Road Board and other organisations in the district. After his retirement to Guildford in 1921 'Glentromie' was owned in turn by the Edgar, Fitzgerald and Nixon families before becoming the property of the Wright family.

References

Murray Nixon, *The Nixon Family History 1914 – 1989*, Printex, Perth, 1989.
Interviews with descendants of the Macpherson brothers.
Inquirer, 20 April 1887.

41. SUMMER HILL

'Summer Hill', north of New Norcia, was pioneered by John Halligan (1840 – 1925) who arrived from Ireland in 1865 at the age of twenty-five years. He had been nominated by a relative, Hugh Hynes, who owned a small property in the Canning district. According to descendants Halligan was employed by the Dempsters. He also worked, until March 1873, as a shepherd at 'Marah', the Benedictine farm near Watheroo. It is possible the Benedictines provided cabaroos or small portable huts for their shepherds. These were in common use in Britain and could be moved easily to fresh pastures. After this time Halligan may have squatted on the land he was to purchase thirteen months later.

'Summer Hill', 2003.
Courtesy Jenny Sinclair.

Granary.
Courtesy Jenny Sinclair.

In April 1874 Halligan acquired a forty-acre block of Crown Land centered around a permanent soakage. The soil on this land was good, but very stony. He fenced his farm with the stones and, in common with other colonial farmers, chopped the trees down.

During the 1870s and 1880s people of non-Catholic religion had to travel to Toodyay or Gingin for their pastoral care. In 1875 Halligan married Mary Jane Woods in Newcastle (Toodyay) at St Stephen's Anglican Church, but later two of their children were buried in Gingin as this was nearer to 'Summer Hill'.

Halligan also held a Special Occupation Lease (SOL) north of New Norcia, part of Donald Macpherson's original pastoral lease of 1845, and in due course received the freehold title. His rise in fortune is typical of several labourers who achieved the status of a successful and influential landholder.

The original three-roomed mud bat cottage erected at 'Summer Hill' had a long room on the shady side, which served as a dairy where shallow pans filled with milk were set for cream. At each end were two narrowing slits in walls, a little above floor level, which acted as cooling devices when hot winds whistled through them. Later as his family grew larger the house was enlarged. The building was faced with stone. Bricks used for the doorways and chimneys were purchased from Halligan's brother-in-law James Sheridan, who made them by hand on his adjoining property.

To provide water for the house and stock Halligan dug a well in the same way as those made by the Benedictines. It was about twelve feet deep and the same width across and lined with stone. This reservoir of water never failed them even during a succession of dry seasons.

In time John Halligan built a shearing shed, granary, solid barn and extensive stables, with a special section for a carriage, of which he was very proud.

Seven of the twelve Halligan children reached adulthood. The eldest, Jane was born in 1879 followed in 1880 by John. Four more were born in quick succession. Mrs Halligan needed help so they nominated Halligan's niece Alicia Halligan as an assisted immigrant. She arrived in 1881 on the understanding that she would sign over to John Halligan the 50 acres that a migrant was entitled to claim.

Within a year Alicia Halligan married a neighbour, John Longman of 'Marlborough' (later known as 'Marbro'). So John Halligan then nominated a nephew named John Halligan, who arrived in 1883. He applied for an immigrant grant of land and was allotted fifty acres (Melbourne Location 886) in 1884.

John Halligan Senior enlarged his property by applying for another Special Occupation Lease of 5500 acres, which became freehold (Melbourne Location 490) some years later. In time he was also owner of 'Tatopini', 'Duck Pool Farm', 'Skibberene', 'Dumpinjerry', 'Marbro' and a property at Carnamah. The two last named were originally owned by relatives by marriage. The value of his land rose when proposals were made to build a railway connecting Perth with Geraldton. The proposed route was not far from 'Summer Hill'. Land was set aside for a railway station at a place named Waddington. An enterprising innkeeper built a hotel there and as a town was envisaged some people settled nearby. In 1889 he leased a further 21,500 acres of land granted to John Waddington of the Midland Railway Company.

John Halligan assumed leadership in this area. In 1891 he called a meeting at 'Summer Hill' to promote a ploughing match on his property, the first to be held in the Victoria Plains district. Judges, participants and committee members were entertained that evening at his home where prizes were presented and three hearty cheers for John Halligan resounded throughout the house.

After the meeting the Victoria Plains Farmers' Association was formed. Halligan was elected as Secretary and the meeting place was at the Waddington Hotel. By popular consent they decided to hold agricultural shows there. This community spirit lasted only a short time.

Stick and stone fencing.
Courtesy Jenny Sinclair.

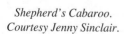

Shepherd's Cabaroo.
Courtesy Jenny Sinclair.

Bishop Salvado objected to the railway going through Mission land and the line was re-routed to the west of New Norcia passing through Mogumber instead. The community activities were then focussed more centrally at Yarrawindah near New Norcia where a school had existed since the 1870s. In 1906 J. Clune gave land there for the building of Yarrawindah Agricultural Hall. A government subsidy enabled the community to erect a fine brick meeting place. It was opened with a three-day programme of sports, horse races, a bazaar and a ball.

By then John Halligan was retiring from public affairs and his sons William and Henry were of an age to take his place. He died in 1925 and was buried in a small cemetery beside the road that passed 'Glentromie' and 'Summer Hill'. His epitaph reads

Life's race well run
Life's work well done
Life's crown well won
Now comes rest.

'Summer Hill' did not remain for long in the family after John Halligan's death. However, subsequent owners recognized the historic value of the farm buildings and several are still in use. They were all maintained in good order and are a rare example of the presentation of an entire complex worthy of the title of 'A Museum of Farm Buildings'.

References
Rica Erickson, *The Victoria Plains*, Lamb Paterson Pty Ltd, Osborne Park, 1971.
Interviews with John Gavin and members of the Longman family.
Notes from Jenny Sinclair.
Summer Hill Farm Precinct Conservation Plan, prepared by Jenny Sinclair and Dorothy Erickson, 2001.

42. WALEBING

'Walebing' has been in the Lefroy family hands since 1846. The brothers Anthony O'Grady Lefroy (1816 – 1897) and Gerald De Courcy Lefroy (1819 – 1878) arrived at Fremantle from Ireland in 1843. While they were disembarking one of their bags was accidentally dropped overboard. It contained all their worldly wealth of 900 gold sovereigns, the equivalent of $90,000 in modern value. Fortunately a sailor dived overboard and retrieved it. He was to become one of their most valued employees.

'Walebing', 2003.
Courtesy Jenny Piercy.

The Lefroys stayed for a year at York with the Burges brothers who agreed to give them a year's experience in farm and pastoral management at the cost of £50 each. This was equivalent to the annual wage of four labourers. At the end of the year they leased 'Spring Hill', a property near Northam where they grazed a flock of sheep and then searched for a suitable area to make a permanent home.

They were acquainted with Captain Scully, a fellow Irishman who was Resident Magistrate of the Toodyay district and had explored beyond his farm at Bolgart. He told them of the Victoria Plains where large areas of pastoral land were open for selections of leases. This country had been explored only a few years before but already most of the land along the Moore River was taken up by shepherds. When Scully was called to Ireland on family business in 1846 the Lefroys leased his farm.

Gerald then explored further north than the Moore River and in December 1846 applied for a large leasehold at Bebano and named the property 'Walebing'. It was agreed that Gerald would manage the Bolgart farm and supervise the flock sent to this lease in the care of a shepherd.

'Walebing' cottage, built c.1852.
Courtesy Lefroy family.

Stables, built 1850s.
Courtesy Lefroy family.

Anthony would remain in Perth where he would seek a position in the Civil Service to help keep them in funds.

Shortly after Gerald settled at Bolgart he had the misfortune to lose his servants' living quarters in a fire, as already mentioned in the account regarding the Bolgart Water Reserve. Before long he had a cottage built of stone and mud at 'Walebing', which was known as the 'Mia', and was busy making other improvements despite a fall in the price of wool. He was courting Elizabeth Brockman, but her father withheld his consent for her marriage for a whole year.

During this period of probation Gerald built a larger cottage of mud brick and stone, employing a Guildford stone mason named Henry Pike in December 1851 to lay the foundations at the cost of threepence a yard, and five shillings a day for laying the mud bricks. The flooring consisted of a cement-like mixture of crushed ant-heap, sand and lime (bought at some cost) in equal proportions. The building was seventeen feet deep with four rooms in a row of the width of twenty, fourteen, ten and eight feet. The roof was of tin (galvanised iron) in flat sheets. He feared it might leak but was reassured on the night he moved in, to hear the rain falling heavily on the roof and not a drop came into the rooms.

Gerald De Courcy Lefroy married Elizabeth Brockman in May 1852. His partnership with his brother was dissolved shortly after. By the next

year Gerald and Elizabeth were sailing to Madras in charge of a cargo of Brockman's horses. After completing that business they sailed to Ireland where they lived until their return to Western Australia in 1860, taking up land in the Southwest.

In the meantime 'Walebing' was managed for Anthony O'Grady Lefroy by John Joyce. Anthony's son Henry Bruce Lefroy (1854 – 1930) was expected to assume management after his return from University studies in England. He was scarcely eighteen years of age when he went to 'Walebing' in 1871. Old John Joyce retired but his son John remained on the pay roll and was to be faithful retainer there for forty-one years.

Soon after H. B. Lefroy took up the reins at 'Walebing' he was nominated by Bishop Salvado as a J.P. They were to become firm friends. He coached a team of Aboriginal cricketers and sponsored the matches in Perth where their skill won universal admiration. He was not prepared to marry until he built a more suitable dwelling for a bride. This homestead was of brick and quarried stone, the beams and floorboards were pit sawn in the Bindoon Forest where sheoak shingles were split as well. Marble fireplaces were imported from Italy, doors and architraves from England. During 1875 and 1877 he employed two ticket-of-leave carpenters, Patrick Byrne and William Hawkins and it is possible that others were expirees known to be working as builders in the district.

The large three-sided house was built around an underground tank to hold water from the roof. This substantial homestead was finished well in time for Henry Bruce Lefroy's marriage to Rose Wittenoom in 1880.

At its peak 'Walebing' included 100,000 acres of pastoral leasehold, some of it held since 1846. Much of this land was transferred to the Midland Railway Company and when these concessions were auctioned in 1908 Lefroy bought 15,000 acres. Pasture development replaced the former open range management of flocks. The land was fenced and shepherds were no longer required. Land was cleared for cropping and sheep numbers reduced from 10,000 to 3,000. As a farm 'Walebing' was still a very large property and was one of the few in Western Australia to remain in the hands of the original pioneers by the year 2000.

H. B. Lefroy had a very distinguished career. He was elected to the Victoria Plains Road Board during 1872-1899 and served as its chairman for twenty years. During 1872-1901 he was elected as a member of the Legislative Assembly for the Moore District. His numerous public duties obliged him to travel frequently between 'Walebing' and Perth. It took three days to make the journey with horse and carriage, with overnight stops at New Norcia and Bindoon. After his father's death in 1897 H. B. Lefroy lived in Perth, leaving the management of 'Walebing' to Steve Sheridan. His Parliamentary duties were suspended during 1901-1904 while he was in London as Agent General for Western Australia. After his return home he was again elected to Parliament during 1911-1921, serving as Premier 1917-1919. He was knighted in 1919 in recognition of his long public service.

References

Cranfield, R. E., From Ireland to Western Australia: the establishment of a branch of a Lefroy family at Walebing, WA, 1842 to 1960, Service Printing Co., Perth, 1960.

G.S. Reid and M. R. Oliver, *The Premiers of Western Australia* , UWA Press, Nedlands, 1982.

Lefroy Diaries, 648A Battye Library.

Correspondence with E.H.B Lefroy.

Resident Magistrates Letter Books. Toodyay, BL. C90 250/1852 re Pike.

43. BERKSHIRE VALLEY

James Clinch's property 'Berkshire Valley' was the most northerly of those listed in the Toodyay district census of 1849. Clinch was born at Berkshire, England in 1815 and arrived in the colony in January 1840 with Frederick Slade, who employed him as a shepherd. By December 1846 he was already an independent farmer and owner of a flock of sheep. In January 1847 he applied for a pastoral lease of 4000 acres near Lefroy's lease at 'Walebing'. He built a one-roomed ram-jam (pise) hut with a dirt floor and a thatched roof. By the end of the year he was carting wheat from his first crop for gristing at Drummond's mill in Toodyay.

'Berkshire Valley', 1998.
Courtesy Hamilton family.

'Berkshire Valley',
side and rear view of
homestead showing the
original stone structure.
Courtesy Hamilton family.

According to the 1849 census there were no women in his household, but it is possible that Clinch employed James Doust as a shepherd. Gerald de Courcy Lefroy mentioned Mrs Doust in his diary entry for 15 November 1850. She lived some distance away and he had sent for her

'Berkshire Valley' Stables restored by the Hamilton family. Photograph: Jenny Piercy, 2003. Courtesy Hamilton family.

to attend his housekeeper Mrs Pell who was in labour and about to give birth to a son. A month later Mrs Pell went to Mrs Doust's aid when her son was born at Walebeing.

James Clinch became independent when he bought 50 acres of freehold land (Melbourne Location 3) in 1850 and added another 10 acres at Kiaka to the west in 1853. He married an immigrant girl named Catherine O'Connell in December the same year.

In 1855 when Resident Magistrate Harris of Toodyay made a routine visit of the Victoria Plains he noted that Clinch had a substantial house of ram-jam construction as well as a neat dairy, and labourers' quarters by the stables. There were stockyards, a kitchen garden and several wells. His fifty acres of wheat were comparable with crops sown by owners of the largest grants of land.

By 1869 after a series of dry years Clinch's washpools were shallow and muddy and were useless for washing sheep before shearing. More wells were sunk by a ticket-of-leave man named Thomas Smith. He began building a shearing shed of bricks which included a trough where sheep could be washed in warm water and then placed in a drying room before shearing. It may also have been used when pigs were killed and then placed in scalding hot water to facilitate the removal of the bristles.

'Berkshire Valley' was a hospitable staging post for the few travellers on their way to Perth or Geraldton, and as a consequence it became an unofficial post office for the collection and despatch of mail. Because some travellers arrived late at night Clinch built a small guesthouse beside the homestead fence.

Undoubtedly he would have had a blacksmith who could assist the travellers with their vehicles, often in need of repairs to the wheels. The roads were rough and the wheels suffered considerable damage. A blacksmith at a wayside stop was as essential in those days as a mechanic

The homestead outbuildings were occupied by the Army during World War II when a Japanese invasion was feared. Courtesy Hamilton family.

at a modern petrol service station. Much strength and skill was required to make the new iron tyres fit a wheel and also to repair the wooden sections. Robert Viveash, an early settler, wrote as early as 1840 to a friend in England who was contemplating sailing to the colony. 'Should you bring a cart out I should advise you not to have the wheels made – but bring the iron work and get them made here as the English wood does not last long in this colony for wheels. The heat makes it shrink so much they soon fall to pieces.'

Clinch also built a double-arch bridge across the brook that resembled one near his old home in England. The footing was of stone and the arches were of burnt brick. He planned the building of a flourmill and granary, with stables, a smithy and workshop near some labourers' quarters. The flour mill, which was driven by steam, had walls of mud brick and random rubble. Apart from the roofing beams and shingles, the timber for the mill's construction was pit sawn. Wooden louvres were placed in the southwest wall for ventilation, while imported glass was used for the windows on the southeast. The bags of wheat were lifted from the wagons to the upper floor by the use of pulleys and hauled inside where the wheat was poured into bins lined with tin to prevent mice from spoiling it. Before being put through the mill the grain was screened in a hopper. Neighbouring farmers were soon bringing their wheat to be milled at 'Berkshire Valley'.

Most of Clinch's buildings were erected in the 1870s by expirees and ticket-of-leave men. In 1872 Bolton was making bricks, while Patrick Byrne worked as a carpenter for six months in 1877 along with John McAllen a plumber. As already mentioned in the story on 'Glentromie' two Chinese tradesmen were employed at 'Berkshire Valley' during 1881-2. A hint of Chinese design is to be seen in some of the brickwork.

Henry Slade in England wrote to Clinch suggesting that when Clinch made his fortune he too could go home to England and live like a gentleman to the end of his days. But Clinch was too happily settled in the colony to contemplate leaving. Between 1871 – 1888 he was a member of the Victoria Plains Road Board, and in 1878 he organised the first Victoria Plains Race Meeting at Berkshire Valley. He also bred horses for the India trade. His last sale of horses was a mob of thirty, driven to Geraldton in 1892 to meet the demands of prospectors bound for the goldfields at Mt Magnet.

At the time of his death in 1899 James Clinch owned 1818 acres of freehold and 41,000 acres of pastoral lease, which were decreased considerably when lands were granted to the Midland Railway Company. His son Alfred sold 'Berkshire Valley' in 1905 to the Benedictines at New Norcia. In 1913 Richard Hamilton, a mine manager from Kalgoorlie-Boulder, bought 'Berkshire Valley' with its outbuildings and 1200 acres of the land. During the 1940s the Army occupied the 'Berkshire Valley' when there were fears of a Japanese invasion.

The Berkshire Valley Museum

In 1968 an earthquake damaged both the mill and the stables. These were faithfully restored by the Hamilton family and with the assistance of the Moora Historical Society a museum was created. Local items of historical interest are displayed inside the museum while larger items such as the old horse-drawn works and bag-lifter, as well as a tyre shrinker, are displayed outdoors.

Among the farm buildings and structures that attract visitors' attention is the guest house for the wayside travellers and the unique double arched bridge. However, perhaps the most interesting building in the complex is that built to house and slaughter the pigs. Warm in winter and cool in summer with every convenience for feeding and managing pigs it compares favourably with any modern pig farm. In recent times it was restored as a guest room.

The museum was open for inspection with due ceremony by Dame Alexandra Hasluck in August 1970. It is owned and maintained by the Hamilton family as a memorial honouring the life and work of James Clinch.

These old farms and homesteads from 'Morby' at Northam to 'Berkshire Valley' at Moora provide an insight into the building methods and lives of colonists as they emerged from the horse age into the revolutionary machine age. Most of them can be viewed from the road and studied as part of a rural museum on a very large scale.

References

Notes by the Hamilton family.
Moora Historical Society. *A sketch of James Clinch of Berkshire Valley.*
Lefroy Diaries, 648A. Battye Library.

'Berkshire Valley Museum', formerly the Flour Mill. Photograph: Jenny Piercy, 2003. Courtesy Hamilton family.

Display of farm tools and corn grinder. Photograph: Jenny Piercy, 2003. Courtesy Hamilton family.

Tyre-shrinker. Photograph: Jenny Piercy, 2003. Courtesy Hamilton family.

CONCLUSION

This account of pioneer farms and families began with 'Morby' at Northam and ends with 'Berkshire Valley' which were settled in 1836 and 1847 respectively. The old winding tracks that linked them were for travellers on foot, on horseback, or in carts. Heavily loaded wagons took a day to go twelve or fifteen miles from one water hole to the next. Present day travellers speed along straighter and wider roads and very few are aware of the historical value of the old farmhouses along the way.

Only four of the old properties remain in the hands of descendants of the original owners – 'Bardeen', 'Culham', New Norcia and 'Walebing'. Some of the owners of the other old farms may be unaware of their early histories, sometimes believing stories, not always based on fact, which were told by old timers. Such stories inspired the writing of this record of the farms and families of the early Toodyay district.

APPENDIX 1

Toodyay District Returns, 30 November 1849
[Where the numbers are small (such as for goats, pigs, oats, rye, maize, potatoes and vineyards) these have been printed in the author's comments which appear in italics.]

Householders names	Males above 12 years	Males below 10 years	Females above 12 years	Females below 12 years	Horses	Horned Cattle	Sheep	Wheat – acres	Barley – acres	Kitchen garden – acres	Green Crops – acres
Frederick SLADE 'Glen Avon'	4	-	4	2	11	110	650	11	-	$\frac{1}{2}$	6
Wife, 1 son, 3 daughters above 12 years and 1 below. He may have employed a married couple with children as well as a single man.											
CHITTY and LEE tenants 'Buckland'	7	5	2	2	36	11	2600	25	6	$\frac{1}{2}$	25
G.E. Chitty, wife, 1 son over 12 years and 3 under 12, 1 daughter. Lee was unmarried. Employed possibly 3 single men and a married couple with 1 son and 1 daughter. Kept 2 goats.											
Abraham MORGAN 'Bardeen'	3	1	2	-	7	30	900	14	5	$\frac{1}{2}$	-
His mother, wife, 1 son. Employed possibly 2 men.											
Joseph CHARLTON 'Windmill Hill'	1	-	-	-	1	-	-	3	-	$\frac{1}{2}$	-
Unmarried, had a small vineyard.											
John MILLS	4	1	1	1	-	-	-	3	-	-	-
Wife, 2 children and 3 employees.											
Messrs LOCKYER "Hampton Farm'											
Thomas Lockyer, wife and son. Joseph Lockyer unmarried. Employees were possibly 2 men and a married couple.											
James WOODWARD Northam	1	-	-	-	-	1	-	-	-	-	-
Licensee of a hotel, had $\frac{1}{4}$ acre vineyard and $\frac{1}{2}$ acres kitchen garden.											
G. WOOLHOUSE Chidlow's employee	1	2	2	1	1	4					
Wife, 2 sons, 1 daughter and a woman who may have been a servant. Kept 4 pigs.											

Name											
William CHIDLOW 'Island Farm'	5	-	2	2	20	200	2100	25	15	$\frac{1}{4}$	8
Wife, 2 daughters. Employees possibly a married couple and 3 men. Grew 2 acres of Rye.											
Fred^k MORRELL 'Morby'	3	2	2	2	6	8	732	6	2	$\frac{3}{4}$	2
Wife, 2 sons, 2 daughters. Employed possibly a married couple and 2 men. Had 20 pigs, 10 goats.											
J.T. COOKE 'Newleyine'	6	2	1	-	10	145	2500	9	-	$\frac{1}{4}$	8
Wife, 2 sons and 5 employees.											
J.B. RIDLEY 'Egoline'	4	-	-	-	3	30	-	-	-	-	-
Employed 3 men.											
William McKNOE 'Jingaling'	3	-	-	-	6	26	350	18	2	-	-
Employed 2 men. Grew $3\frac{1}{2}$ acres oats.											
WHITFIELD G.M & T 'Knockdominie'	4	-	-	-	6	110	1000	12	2	-	24
Employed 2 men. Had 6 goats.											
Messrs GOOCH 'Mountain Farm'	6	-	-	-	5	-	2000	9	2	-	$\frac{1}{2}$
Employed 3 or 4 men.											
John BRITT near 'Culham'	2	1	1	-	-	9	-	3	1	$\frac{1}{4}$	-
Wife, 1 son. Employed 1 man. Had 11 pigs.											
Charles BATES =BETTS, lessee of Byrne's grant	3	-	1	2	1	-	800	-	-	1	2
Wife, 2 daughters. Employed 2 men. Grew 2 acres wheat. Had 11 pigs.											
Robert WATERS 'Barn Elms'	2	2	1	3							
Wife, 2 sons, 3 daughters. Employed 1 man. Grew $\frac{1}{2}$ acre potatoes.											
James FERGUSON Farmer, 'Barn Elms'	-	-	-	-	6	-	-	11	-	-	-
Son of Alex Sr. Had 12 pigs.											
Alex FERGUSON 'Barn Elms' lessee Blacksmith	4	2	3	2	-	-	-	-	-	-	-
Wife, 2 sons and 2 ??? 12 years, 1 daughter and possibly 1 married couple and child.											
John DELAMORE at 'Hawthornden'	2	3	-	1							
Carpenter, widower, 1 or 2 sons below 12 years, 2 daughters.											
Thomas HICKS	2	-	1	-	-	-	-	-	-	-	-
Shepherd, employed possibly by Drummond.											

Name											
Charles HARPER 'Nardie', lessee	4	1	2	3	8	74	-	6	3	$\frac{1}{4}$	10

Wife, 1 son, 2 daughters. Employed possibly a married couple, 2 men, one being Chinese.

Name											
James DRUMMOND 'Hawthornden'	8	2	2	-	11	40	1900	22	2	$\frac{1}{2}$	10

Wife, 3 sons, who employed several men including J. Cook, J. Green, P. Ambrose, Thomis Davis and wife.

| Charles GEE1 at Toodyay | - | 1 | - | 2 | - | - | - | - | - | - | |

Policeman and wife.

| William ROSER Toodyay farmer | 1 | 1 | 2 | 2 | 8 | - | - | 9 | 3 | $\frac{1}{4}$ | - |

Wife, 1 son, 3 daughters, one of them above 12 years. Had 7 pigs.

| Thos HARRINGTON Small farmer Toodyay | 1 | - | - | - | | | | 10 | 15 | $\frac{1}{4}$ | |

He employed Thomas Dixon, not listed. Had 25 pigs and 6 goats.

| F. GEE (=? Frederick Walter) Toodyay | 3 | - | 1 | 3 | - | 3 | - | - | - | - | - |

? wife and family.

| F. WHITFIELD Jr 'Nunyle' | 4 | 2 | 1 | - | 2 | 57 | | 20 | 4 | _ | |

Wife, 2 sons. Employed 3 labourers. Had 4 pigs.

| Thos G. COOK | 4 | 3 | 1 | 2 | 3 | 57 | 850 | 20 | 4 | $\frac{1}{4}$ | - |

Wife, 3 sons, 2 daughters, worked for Slade and then farmed at Wongamine before leasing 'Roesland'.

| Wm DODD 'Knockdominie' | 1 | - | 1 | - | 1 | - | - | 2 | $2\frac{1}{2}$ | - | |

Wife. Lessee at Knockdominie and then to Glen Avon.

| Charles CLINCH 'Nunyle' | 3 | 1 | 1 | - | 6 | 6 | 840 | 9 | 6 | $1\frac{1}{2}$ | - |

? lessee, unmarried. Employed possibly one man and a married couple with a boy.

| John WHEELOCK tenant farmer | 3 | 4 | 2 | 1 | 1 | 67 | - | 40 | 36 | - | - |

Wife, 4 sons, 1 daughter. Employed possibly 1 man and a married couple.

| H. JOHNSON employee | 1 | - | - | - | - | - | - | - | - | $\frac{1}{4}$ | 4 |

Perhaps John Henry Johnson, blacksmith at Glen Avon. Had 6 pigs.

| George SHEPHERD | 1 | - | - | - | 1 | - | - | 12 | - | $\frac{1}{4}$ | - |

Unmarried employee.

| James CROAL | 1 | - | - | - | - | - | - | - | - | - | - |

Unmarried. Shepherd?

| Wm. MEARES | 1 | - | - | - | - | - | - | - | - | - | - |

Unmarried. Shepherd?

Name											
James SINCLAIR 'Dumbarton'	4	2	2	4	5	47	400	16	3	-	$1/4$
Wife, 2 sons, 3 daughters and relatives, the Glass family. Had 30 pigs and 2 goats.											
F. WHITFIELD Sr 'Knockdominie'	1	-	-	-	3	23	-	-	-	$1/4$	-
Widower. Retired recluse.											
Lionel LUKIN 'Deepdale'	3	3	3	4	23	63	1150	-	3	1	3
Wife, 3 sons, 4 daughters. Employed William Carroll and his wife and 1 man. Had 1 pig and 3 goats.											
S.P. PHILLIPS 'Culham' horse breeder	6	2	3	3	120	30		30		2	30
Wife, employed J. Ryder, J. Thomas, Walker, T. O'Neill with wife, 2 sons, 4 daughters and another man. Grew 5 acres oats and had 61 pigs.											
E. MACKINTOSH 'Coondle' and 'Erandyne'	6	-	2	-	12	110	4150	37	5	-	20
Wife. Employees included 5 men and 1 woman (possibly a married couple and 4 men).											
G de C. LEFROY' 'Walebing'	7	-	-	-	111	113	3201	-	-	-	-
Employed Dollard and Higgins, Clark, 2 Parkhurst boys and a black cook.											
James CLINCH 'Berkshire Valley'	6	-	-	-	6	200	3600	8	4	$1/4$	4
Employed 5 men. Had 20 pigs.											
Ed. BEERE Bolgart lessee	4	1	3	2	2	21	900	11	-	1	-
Wife, 1 son, 4 daughters. Employed 3 men. Had 8 pigs.											
M. CLARKSON Toodyay	2	3	2	1	1	-	500	-	-	-	-
Wife, 4 sons (1 an adult), 2 daughters (1 an adult).											
Wm HERBERT Toodyay innkeeper	1	1	1	2	-	-	-	-	-	-	-
Wife, 1 son, 2 daughters.											
John HERBERT Toodyay	3	1	1	2	1	18	-	2	-	-	-
Wife, 1 son, 1 daughter. Employed 2 men and 1 girl possible relative.											
Wm CRIDDLE 'Stanton Spring'	3	1	1	2	8	3	-	8	-	-	-
Wife, 2 sons, 2 daughters. Employed 2 men. Had 11 pigs.											
Wm CARROLL 'Deepdale'	2	-	1	-	-	-	-	$2^{1}/_{4}$	-	-	-
Small farmer and labourer. Wife and a man.											

	C1	C2	C3	C4	C5	C6	C7	C8	C9	C10	C11
Ed. CONLIN Toodyay	4	-	-	-	3	1800	-	-	-	-	-
Unmarried pastoralist. Employed 3 men.											
D. MACPHERSON 'The Byeen' tenant	10	3	1	-	11	38	6000	13	3	$\frac{1}{2}$	6
Wife, 3 sons. Employed 9 men including G. Gladwell and John Patton.											
Isaac DOUST ? 'The Carroll' ? employee	2	3	2	1	-	6	-	11	-	$\frac{1}{2}$	-
Wife, 3 sons, 2 daughters. Employed a married couple. Grew 6 acres oats.											
John DAVIDSON Victoria Plains	5	-	-	-	12	-	2340	5	2	$\frac{1}{2}$	1
Pastoralist. Employed 4 men.											
James DOUST 'Berkshire Valley'	1	1	1	1	-	-	-	-	-	-	-
Wife, 1 son, 1 daughter. Employed by Clinch.											
R.C. Mission 'New Norcia'	7	-	-	-	4	29	1886	20	4	-	-
5 monks and W. Fowler and J.M. Butler. Had 59 pigs and 1 goat.											
Robt. De BURGH 'Egoline', lessee	3	1	2	3	1	13	4	31	-	$\frac{3}{4}$	-
Wife, 1 son, 1 daughter. Employed 1 man and ? a married couple with 2 daughters.											
John WALKER 'Baylie Farm'	2	1	-	-	7	9	988	15	-	1	-
Tenant? Employed 1 man and 1 boy.											
TOTALS 58 households	188	59	63	52	384	1976	46,646	534	$100\frac{1}{2}$	$15\frac{1}{2}$	$205\frac{1}{2}$

APPENDIX 2

Aborigines listed by the Resident Magistrate of Toodyay F. Whitefield in March 1840, as recipients of rations. *Denotes women who also received blankets.

Men	Women	Boys	Girls	Residences	Character
Narrain	*Berrigan	-	-	Mr Habgood's farm	Good. This means they have not committed any recent depredations
	*Youligar	-	-	"	-
Thacker	*Nalgan	-	-	"	-
Carrabunga alias Tom	-	-	-	Ridley's	
Quitwood alias Bonaparte	Nannigen	1	-	"	
Annapwirt	Nalgamma	1	-	Heal's	Bad. Murderer of Chidlow and Jones
Melap	Welbannan	1	2	"	
Winglewood (Charlie)	Walligan	1	2	"	Good
Carrypirt (Captain)	-	-	-		
Werite	Minamung	-	-	"	Bad. Stealing goats and wheat
	Merringam (old woman)				
Mogan	-		-	Mr Cook's	Good
Dulap	-	-	-	Major Nairn's	Bad
Walgurwood	*Darganna	4	1	Mr Whitfield's	Good
Catting Wood	*Narrane	1	-	-	Good
Mangap	Nitingal	-	-	Mr Drummond	Good
Melick	Yadang	1	-	"	Good
Nalligan (Alluck)	-	-	-	"	Good
Yarringan	Yandebone	1	-	"	Good
Bindal	*Gimmegom	1	-	"	Good
Cowgan	-	-	-	"	Good

Men	Women	Boys	Girls	Residences	Character
Belgap	Dwabban	-	-	Mr Lukin	Good
	Magom	-	-	"	Good
	*Buggegon	2	2	"	Good
Dulebah	Noon dang	1	-	"	Good
Dewar	*Noon dally	2	1	"	Good
Nannepirt	-	-	-	Capt.Pratt	Bad. Rape
Cooricap	*Yandebung	2	-	"	Good
	*Nevagon	1	-	"	Good
Yourab	Doonbong	-	-	Mr Leake	Bad. Stole 20 sheep. Lately from Capt.Pratt
Niam	-	-	-	"	
Wobat	Midigan	2	1	"	
	Ninegan	-	-	"	
Hooran	-	-	-	Capt Scully	Good
Gooridebong	-	-	-	"	Good
Namip	*Yoondanna	4	-	Mr Phillips	Good
Dulebah	Noonda	1	-	"	Good
Mocop	Goola	1	1	"	Good
Total 32	28	31	10		

APPENDIX 3

This list of men of convict origin engaged in building during the colonial years was compiled from a file in the Battye Library on Employees of Ticket-of-Leave Men (Western Australian Biographical Index,WABI). Some have been verified by family records of farm journals and payment of wages.

The list includes some labourers who were known to assist the building tradesmen. The places of employment are given to homesteads in the districts of Toodyay and Victoria Plains. The asterisks denote those who worked at 'Buckland'.

*Charles Adams (7609) labourer

William Allen (4844) carpenter at 'Maisemore'

*Thomas Ashmore (8476) carpenter

Robert Baker (6826) brickmaker at 'Glendearg' at Toodyay with Hasell

Edward Baldock (9070) bricklayer and brickmaker at 'Glendearg'

Mark Barnett (9073) shingle splitter at 'Rose Valley'

Henry Beard (4494) Toodyay

Henry Bolton (6526) brickmaker at 'Berkshire Valley'

*John Bonsor (728) brickmaker, employed by many colonists

*Michael Bowen (2524) carter and labourer

Thomas Broadley (8489) brickmaker, sawyer, with Hasell at Toodyay

*Peter Brehart (6521) at 'Coondle', 'Katrine', 'Buckland' and Esperance

Henry Brocklesby (9090) carpenter at Connor's Mill and also as a shipwright at Geraldton

George Brown (8504) shingle splitter with George Hasell at Toodyay and at 'Culham'

William Butler (9103) bricklayer at 'Glentromie'

Patrick Byrne (9677) carpenter and shingle splitter at 'Glentromie', 'Berkshire Valley' and 'Buckland'

Robert Carter (4974) carpenter

Peter Casey (8822) bricklayer with Hasell at Toodyay

John Challinor (7654) builder at 'Buckland'

Richard Collin (5658) bricklayer

James Cook (6547) sawyer at 'Hawthornden'

John Danks (6000) labourer

Herbert Davis (8248) sawyer with W.G. Leeder and at Connor's Mill

John Davis (7969) sawyer at 'Katrine'

John Dorren (?5370) Dorrington, alias Tracey, mason

Alex Fagan (317) stone cutter at 'Culham'

James Foley (2040) carter

William Fox (4994) carpenter, sawsmith

William Gater (7417) brickmaker at 'The Byeen'. To Sydney 1873

John Greenhalgh (7705) glassblower at 'Katrine'

George Henry Hasell (1225) brickmaker and building contractor

William Hawkins (9760) carpenter and joiner at 'Walebing'

John Hinton (7446) brickmaker at 'Hawthornden'

James Hodgkinson (6884) brickmaker and sawyer at 'Buckland' and Wyening

James Holden (4500) brickmaker at 'Bardeen'

George Holloway (7434) builder and sawyer at 'Buckland'

Thomas Johnson (7737) brickmaker with Hasell and at 'Glen Avon'

William Johnson (6460) engineer at 'Hawthornden'

James Kelly (?) at 'The Byeen'

George Kent (8911) quarryman at 'Roesland'

John Kitson (286) engineer with J. Cousins at Bejoording

John Langham (7182) bricklayer at 'Buckland' and Esperance. To South Australia
1876

John McAllen (9503) plumber and carpenter at 'Berkshire Valley'

Bernard McCabe (4457) carpenter with Thomas Smith, Toodyay

Frederick McDiarmid (4797) carpenter with Thomas Smith of Toodyay

Michael Macnamara (5706) brickmaker at Connors Mill

Thomas Martin (5729) carpenter with Thomas Smith of Toodyay

Jesse Moore (3838) brickmaker with Hasell of Toodyay

John Murray (8641) (alias Bernard Lee Crampton) woodturner and carpenter at
'Roesland'

John Powell (8677) blacksmith, whitesmith, worked with Bonsor

Charles Reilly (8117) brickmaker with Bonsor

John Richardson (6089) carpenter at Connor's Mill

James Riley (2015) brickmaker at 'Barn Elms'

John Riley (5851) brickmaker and plasterer with Hasell at Toodyay

William Robinson (7234) blacksmith at Toodyay, 'Rose Hill'

James Rogers (3047) stonemason

James Rogers (3281) shingle splitter

Job Shenton (6447) timber splitter and carter at Victoria Plains

Roger Scally (2191) carpenter at 'Egoline'

?Henry Smith (?8418) sawyer at 'Bardeen'

John Smith (4006) plasterer with John Britt and Hasell

John Smith (9295) bricklayer and builder for Monger at Toodyay

John Smith (7859) carpenter for W. Smith at Toodyay

Robert Smith (8702) shingle splitter at 'Buckland'

Thomas Smith (2864) glazier at 'Buckland'

William Smith (one of several expirees of this name who worked on buildings in
Toodyay and the Victoria Plains) as bricklayer and plasterer for Res. Mag.
W.J. Clifton

Dan Stevenson (10052) carpenter at 'Glentromie'

Thomas Storey (9307) tin and coppersmith

Thomas Sylvester (9008) for Thomas Smith of Toodyay

James Taylor (7567) at 'Glentromie'

James Ware (9037) carpenter and joiner, worked for John Weasley

John Weasley (9605) builder, bricklayer and mason at 'Buckland' and 'Katrine'. To London January 1878

Joseph Webb (7889) carpenter and cooper for Monger at Toodyay

Charles Webster (alias Dempster) colonial prisoner, at 'Newleyine'

Esau Wetherall (54) stone mason, Toodyay, worked on many buildings

Henry Whitaker (4669) carpenter and joiner, built Granny Clarkson's home. ?worked for James Drummond Jr

John Wilding (3558) engineer and wheelwright at 'Bardeen'

William Willets (7306) sawyer at 'Buckland'

John Wilson a quarrier (one of several convicts of this name worked at Toodyay)

Joseph Wilson (8456) tinsmith, worked for Weasley

Godfrey Woolnough (291) plasterer at 'Roesland'.

INDEX

Illustrations are indicated with **bold page numbers**. Names of vessels are in *italics*.

Northam 3, 19, 22, 24, 26, 53, 55, 76, 88,
    106, 116, 123, 128, 132, 133, 155,
    162
Northam Advertiser 14
Northam Agricultural Society 30
Northam Race Club 30
Northam Road Board 30, 34
North West 64, 76, 81

O

Oakabella 34, 80
Oakfield 35
Oaklands 47, 52, 54
O'Connell, Catherine 160
O'Dea (expiree) 102
Olive Farm 90
O'Neill, Thomas 94, 99, 101, 102
Orient 133
Orleans Farm 123, 124, **124**
Osborne, Charles 120

P

Padbury and Loton 150
Padbury, Walter 9, 102, 108, 150
Parkhurst boys 102, 133
Parliament 158
Parmelia 78, 84, 85, 116, 117
Pastoral industry xi
Pastoral leases 7, 9, 125, 147
Pearling 65
Pell, Mrs 160
Pensioner Guards and Cottages 19, 20,
    22, 64
Pensioners Village 20, 22
Perl, (Peril) William 95
Perth 73, 79, 81, 94, 100, 101, 104, 111,
    117, 142, 153, 157, 160
Perth Gazette 5, 6, 49
Phillips family 104, **104**
Phillips, Fanny 27
Phillips, Mrs 64
Phillips, Samuel Pole and family 7, 27,
    44, 64, 65, 67, 69, 73, 81, 82, 85, 88,
    91, 94, 98, 99, 100, 101, 102, 103,
    104, 105, 106, 107, 108, 114, 118,
    122, 125, 133, 134, 138
Pidcock, W H Rev 106, 107
Piggot, Benjamin 39
Pike, Henry 156

Pinjarra 95
Plaimars Ltd 135
Plantagenet 111
Police 16, 19, 21, 22
Police Barracks 17, 20
Police, Colonial 19
Powell, John 138
Pownall, G P Rev 44, 45, 106
Pratt, Charles and family and Granny
    Pratt 35, 36, 37
Presbyterian 116
Pritchard (expiree) 102
Pritchard, Joe 120, 123
Proclamation of Settlement 1
Protector of Natives 144
Purkis, Frederick 26
Pyrton 98

Q

Quigley 88
Quinlan, Timothy F 68

R

Railways 73, 104, 124, 153
Ralph, Edward 122, 124
Range, The 83
Recreation Grounds 74, 82
Registrar General 69
Register of Historical Places 74
Reilly, Charles 39
Resident Magistrate 44, 80, 81, 91, 132,
    149, 155, 160
Richardson, John 37, 39, 67, 80
Ridley, Charles Dawson and Son 32
Riley, Bishop 107
Riley, James 91
River House 29, 30
Road Boards 22, 67, 86, 105, 135,
Robert, William 51
Roe family 80, 81, 99, 100
Roebourne 42, 65
Roesland 80, 81
Rolands, Robert 69
Rome 142
Ross 138
Rottnest 36
Rowlands, Robert 69
Royal Humane Society 102
Royal Oak 17

Tatopini 153
Taylor, James 148
Telegraph 142
Telephone (exchange) 94, 123
Temperance Hall 125
Tennis clubs 126, 129, 134
Thomson, J G 100, 101
Threshing machine 59
Throssell, George 88
Ticket-of-Leave men 17, 19, 39, 41, 42,
    44, 55, 67, 77, 79, 80, 86, 89, 93, 94,
    100, 116, 122, 142, 148, 157, 160,
    161
Timber mills 39
Tomghin 5
Tomson, John and wife 121, 122
Toodyay Agricultural Society 55, 80
Toodyay Brook 3, 5, 90, 94, 99, 102
Toodyay Convent 68
Toodyay Convict Hiring Depot 17, 19
Toodyay district census (1849) 159
Toodyay Education Board 50, 67, 105
Toodyay ford 16
Toodyay Historical Society 74
Toodyay Municipal Council 67
Toodyay Museum 104
Toodyay (Newcastle) cemetery **70**
Toodyay Northam and Victoria Plains
    Agricultural Society 20, 27, 55, 105
Toodyay Police Barracks 19
Toodyay Road Committee 44
Toodyay Road Board 22, 50, 56, 60, 67,
    81, 82, 86, 103, 105, 109, 113, 130,
    135
Toodyay schools 126
Toodyay settlers 58
Toodyay Shire Council 74, 124, 130
Toodyay Tourist Bureau 68
Toodyay Town Council 22, 67, 124
Toodyay town site 6, 16
Toodyay Valley xi, 5, 6, 22, 64, 66, 72,
    79, 84, 85, 86, 90, 91, 93, 106, 111,
    121
Toodyay Valley Church (Culham) 106
Toodyay West 22
Torres, Bishop 144, 145
Towler, Judd ('Batty') 95, 123
Town Council (Newcastle) 22
Tranby 55, 78, 79

Tranby 3
Travers, Ron 120
Turner, Nancy 52
Twine, James and family 55, 56, **56**, 62

V
Val d'Esperance (Hope Valley) 53
Van Diemen's Land 1
Vettersburgh Hotel 1890's **96**
Vetter family 95, 96
Vetters winery **96**
Vettersberg 95
Victoria Hotel 86
Victoria Plains 7, 9, 16, 44, 67, 85, 86,
    112, 120, 122, 133, 134, 147, 149,
    153, 155, 160
Victoria Plains Farmers Association 153
Victoria Plains Race Meeting 162
Victoria Plains Road Board 86, 135, 144,
    149, 150, 158, 162
Vigors, B U 100
Vine Cottage 37, 38, 81, 83, 86, 88
Viveash, Lionel 27
Viveash, Robert 161
Viveash, Samuel Henry wife and family
    27, 64, 65
Viveash, Simeon wife Mary and family
    41, 42, 45, 56
Viveash, S W Dr 41, 55, 111

W
Waddington Hotel 153
Waddington John 153
Wakeford 104
Walebing 133, 134, 155-158, **155, 156,
    157**, 159, 160, 164
War Veterans Settlement Scheme 120
Warren, Alex 17
Water Reserve 100
Waters 94
Waters, Elizabeth Jane 62
Waters, Robert and family 90, 91, 94
Waters, Robert Betts 90, 91
Waters, Sarah Susan 61
Waters, Thomas and family 5, 6, 90, 91,
    94
Watheroo 142, 151
Wattening 6, 99, 101, 124, 125-126, 127,
    128, 129, 131